MOTIVATOR

In Sync 1

Nick Beare

PEARSON
Longman

In Sync 1 Motivator

Authorized adaptation from the United Kingdom edition, entitled *Upbeat*, first edition, published by Pearson Education Limited publishing under its Longman imprint. Copyright © 2009.

American English adaptation, published by Pearson Education, Inc. Copyright © 2011.

Pearson Education, 10 Bank Street, White Plains, NY 10606, USA

Staff credits: The people who made up the *In Sync* team, representing editorial, production, design, and manufacturing, are Margaret Antonini, Danielle Belfiore, Iris Candelaria, Aerin Csigay, Dave Dickey, Ann France, Lisa Ghiozzi, Emily Lippincott, Leslie Patterson, Stella Reilly, Mary Rich, Barbara Sabella, Donna Schaffer, Julie Schmidt, Mairead Stack, Jennifer Stem, Katherine Sullivan, Jane Townsend, Paula Van Ells, Lauren Weidenman, and Adina Zoltan.

Text composition: TSI Graphics
Text font: Helvetica Neue 10/17

ISBN-13: 978-0-13-254785-7
ISBN-10: 0-13-254785-6

PEARSON LONGMAN ON THE **WEB**

Pearsonlongman.com offers online resources for teachers. Access our Companion Websites, our online catalog, and our local offices around the world.

Visit us at **pearsonlongman.com**.

Printed in the United States of America
1 2 3 4 5 6 7 8 9 10—V012—15 14 13 12 11

Photo credits: All original photography by TSI Graphics and Pearson Education Limited/Gareth Boden. Cover Shutterstock.com; Page 2 (1) Alex Berliner/BEI/Rex Features, (2) Henry Lamb/BEI/Rex Features, (3) AP Images/Dan Steinberg, (4) AP Images/Michael Mariant, (5) Sipa Press/Rex Features, (6) AP Images/SIPA/Zak Brian, (7) Jeff Kravitz/WireImage/Getty Images; 6 (left) Shelly Perry/iStockphoto.com, (right) Comstock Images/PunchStock; 17 (David) BananaStock/PunchStock, (Susana) BananaStock/PunchStock, (Alice) Digital Vision/PunchStock, (Alfonso) BananaStock/PunchStock, (James) BananaStock/PunchStock, (Lucy) Westend61/PunchStock, (Julie) Thinkstock Royalty-Free, (Neil) Thinkstock Royalty-Free, (Davina) BananaStock/PunchStock, (Laila) BananaStock/PunchStock, (Jack) Polka Dot/PunchStock, (Emma) Radius/PunchStock, (Craig) Digital Vision/PunchStock, (Daniel) Thinkstock Royalty-Free, 22 (Max) Justin Horrocks/iStockphoto.com, (Lorna) Image Source/PunchStock, (Tony) Jacob Wackerhausen/iStockphoto.com, (Andy) Jacom Stephens/iStockphoto.com, (Gia) Nikolay Mamluke/iStockphoto.com, (Andrea) iStockphoto.com; 24 (top) ImageState/PunchStock, (bottom) Thinkstock Royalty-Free; 27 (left) Thinkstock Royalty-Free, (right) Blend Images/PunchStock; 28 BananaStock/PunchStock; 38 (top) Jack Carey/Alamy, (bottom) AP Images/Amy Sancetta; 39 Digital Vision/PunchStock; 51 AP Images/Jennifer Graylock; 52 (1) Image Source/PunchStock, (2) RubberBall/Punchstock, (3) Image100/PunchStock, (4) iStockphoto.com, (5) Bruce Laurance/Getty Images; 53 (left) Stephan Hoerold/iStockphoto.com, (middle) Thinkstock Royalty-Free, (right) Thinkstock Royalty-Free; 57 PhotoDisc/PunchStock; 61 (top) Yoshikazu Tsuno/AFP/Getty Images, (bottom) Matthew Simmons/WireImage/Getty Images.

Illustration credits: Illustrations throughout by Beehive Illustration.
Artists: Ray and Corinne Burrows; Wes Lowe; Ian West; Martin Sanders; Mike Lacey.

Contents

1A Celebrity soccer team

1 Look at the photos and unscramble the names. Then use the names and the the words in the box to complete the conversations. Write how old each star is.

- My • your • he • her (×2) • She's • ~~she~~ • is
- are • How • Who's • What's • ~~old~~ • name

1 rancemo adzi
born 8/30/1972

2 éboyenc
born 9/4/1981

3 qireune agseisli
born 5/8/1975

4 lahiyr fudf
born 9/28/1987

Who's ¹ _she_?
She's ² _Cameron Diaz_.
How ³ _old_ is she?
She's ⁴ _____.

⁵ _____ her name?
Her name's ⁶ _____.
⁷ _____ old is she?
She's ⁸ _____.

⁹ _____ he?
He's ¹⁰ _____.
How old is ¹¹ _____?
He's ¹² _____.

What's ¹³ _____ name?
Her name's ¹⁴ _____.
How old is she?
¹⁵ _____ ¹⁶ _____.

5 ykile nugemoi
born 5/28/1968

6 ihmalce lspehp
born 6/30/1985

7 naengail oijel
born 6/4/1975

Who's she?
She's ¹⁷ _____.
How old ¹⁸ _____ she?
¹⁹ _____ ²⁰ _____.

What's ²¹ _____ name?
My name's ²² _____.
How old ²³ _____ you?
I'm ²⁴ _____.

What's your ²⁵ _____?
²⁶ _____ name's ²⁷ _____.
How old are you?
I'm ²⁸ _____.

2 Write the first letter of each first name in the boxes below. Then rearrange the letters to find the last name of the team captain.

| c | | | | | | |

The captain is _____.

2

Copyright © 2011 by Pearson Education, Inc. Permission granted to photocopy for classroom use.

People puzzle!

Read the information about volunteers at the health club and complete the table.

	First name	Last name	Zip code	Phone number	Age	Volunteer days
1	Jackie					*Monday*
2	Peter					_____, _____
3		Jones				_____, _____
4		Meakin				_____, _____

Mrs. K. Jones   16 Pond Road, Tampa, FL 33601   813–555–0102

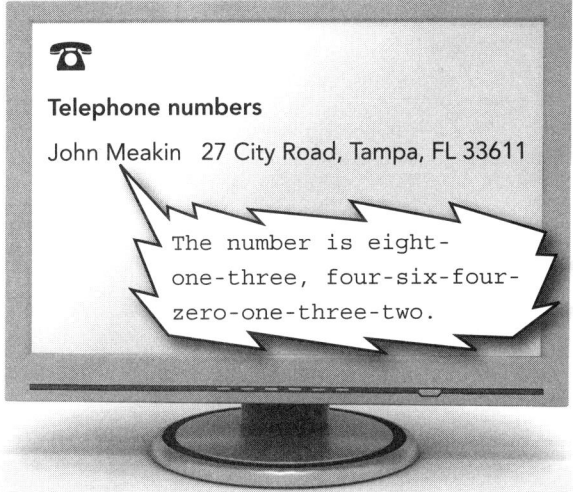

☎

Telephone numbers

John Meakin   27 City Road, Tampa, FL 33611

The number is eight-one-three, four-six-four-zero-one-three-two.

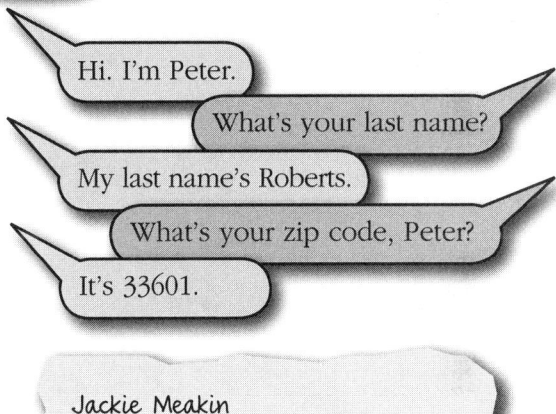

Hi. I'm Peter.

What's your last name?

My last name's Roberts.

What's your zip code, Peter?

It's 33601.

Jackie Meakin
27 City Road, Tampa, Fl 33614

Mrs. Jones, what's your first name?

Karen.

★ **Karen is thirty-one today!** ★

Party at
*16 Pond Road,
Tampa, FL 33601*

How old is John?

He's 17, and Jackie is 16.

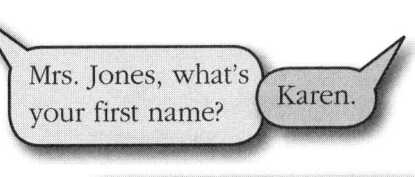

Name: P. Roberts

Age: 25

Jackie
☎ 813-555-0144

Peter
☎ 813-555-2287

Health Club: Volunteer's Calendar

M	T	W	T	F	S	S
1	2	3	4	5	6	7
Jackie	PR	KJ	John	PR	KJ	John

1c Musicians around the world

1 Read about the musicians. Look at the map and draw a line from the musicians to their towns.

1
A: Where are The Toon Boys from?
B: They're from Newcastle.
A: Where's Newcastle?
B: It's in England.

2
A: Where are Mobile Tones from?
B: They're from Cadiz, Spain.

3
A: Where is Fernando Santos from?
B: He's from Lisbon.
A: Where's Lisbon?
B: It's in Portugal.

4
A: Hi! I'm Natalia Alessi.
B: Are you from Russia?
A: No, I'm from Brindisi, Italy.

5
A: Who is Marek Kopolski?
B: He's a singer from Gdansk.
A: Is Gdansk in Russia?
B: No, it isn't. It's in Poland.

6
A: Are you Green Dream?
B: Yes, we are. We're from Nantes.
A: Is Nantes in France?
B: Yes, it is!

2 Write the letter that is next to each town. Rearrange the letters to find the mystery country. Then complete the poster on the right.

[R] [ ] [ ] [ ] [ ] [ ]

Come to the

One World Festival

in _____

Consolidation 1

Words, words, words!

1 Add words to the chart. Use words beginning with *t*, *f*, and *s*.

	First letter	Country	Nationality	Numbers 1–10	Numbers 11–19	Numbers 20–100	Days of the week
1	*t*	Turkey	Turkish	two three ten	twelve thirteen	twenty 1 _____	Tuesday 2 _____
2	*f*	France	3 _____	four 4 _____	fourteen fifteen	5 _____ fifty	Friday
3	*s*	Spain	6 _____	7 _____ 8 _____	9 _____ 10 _____	11 _____ 12 _____	13 _____ 14 _____

2 Read the clues and complete the crossword.

Across   1 a country   2 a number   3 a number   4 a country   5 a number

Down   3 a number   6 a day of the week   7 a country   8 a number   9 a country   10 a day of the week

Who are they?

Student A

Boy X and Girl Y are students at the Quick English school in Chicago. Ask Student B these questions and complete your information about the two students.

About Boy X
What's his name?   What's his address?
What's his phone number?

About Girl Y
How old is she?   Where's she from?
What's her zip code?

Boy X

This is _____.
He's 17. He's from Chile.
His address in the U.S.
is _____. His
zip code is 60605.
His phone number is
_____.

This is Sandra. She's
_____. She's
from _____.
Her address in the U.S.
is 96 Greendale Street,
Chicago, IL. Her zip code
is _____.
Her phone number is 312-268-8115.

Girl Y

✂ -

Student B

Boy X and Girl Y are students at the Quick English school in Chicago. Ask Student A these questions and complete your information about the two students.

About Boy X
How old is he?   Where's he from?
What's his zip code?

About Girl Y
What's her name?   What's her address?
What's her phone number?

Boy X

This is Pedro. He's
_____. He's
from _____.
His address in the U.S.
is 40 Longwood Street,
Chicago, IL. His zip code
is _____. His phone number is
312-555-7720.

This is _____.
She's 14. She's from
Poland. Her address in
the U.S. is _____.
Her zip code is
60605.
Her phone number is _____.

Girl Y

2A Mystery objects

1 What are these? Cross out the letters for the objects in the pictures. Make an extra word with the other letters.

			Picture word	Extra word
1		L̶B̶R̶G̶A̶P̶A̶E̶S̶	*apples*	*bag*
2		A M C W A C H A R T E	_____	_____
3		A N R E K S H T E S A	_____	_____
4		Y S N P S K E E	_____	_____
5		S O T O H I S B R K	_____	_____

2 Write questions and answers with words from Exercise 1.

1 *What are these?*      *They're apples.*

2 _____ ?      _____ .

3 _____ ?   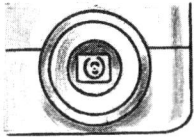   _____ .

4 _____ ?   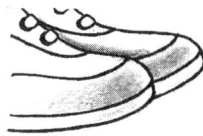   _____ .

5 _____ ?      _____ .

2B What color is that?

Match the people with the objects. Unscramble the colors. Write sentences.

1 Darren

2 Natalie

3 Her friend

4 His brothers

5 His sisters

kpin _____

rgya _____

robnw _____

cbkal   *black*

lpuepr _____

1 *Darren's phone is black.*

2 _____.

3 _____.

4 _____.

5 _____.

2c How much is it?

Student A

1 Ask Student B questions and complete the prices on the menu.

A: *How much is a cheese sandwich?*   B: *It's $4.50.*

Food/Snacks		Drinks	
Chicken sandwich	$5.50	Soda	75¢
Cheese sandwich	$4.50	Bottled water	
Burger	$3.75	Orange juice	$1.50
Hot dog		Hot chocolate	
Potato chips	75¢	Tea	$1.00
Ice cream		Coffee	

2 Look at the total prices and add the missing information.

1
Tea	$1.00
_____	_____
TOTAL	$4.75

2
_____	_____
Orange juice	$1.50
TOTAL	$6.00

3
Chicken sandwich	$5.50
_____	_____
Soda	75¢
TOTAL	$7.00

✂ -

Student B

1 Ask Student A questions and complete the prices on the menu.

A: *How much is a chicken sandwich?*   B: *It's $5.50.*

Food/Snacks		Drinks	
Chicken sandwich	$5.50	Soda	
Cheese sandwich	$4.50	Bottled water	$1.00
Burger		Orange juice	
Hot dog	$1.75	Hot chocolate	$1.50
Potato chips		Tea	
Ice cream	$2.00	Coffee	$1.50

2 Look at the total prices and add the missing information.

1
Ice cream	$2.00
_____	_____
TOTAL	$2.75

2
_____	_____
Hot chocolate	$1.50
TOTAL	$3.25

3
Cheese sandwich	$4.50
_____	_____
Bottled water	$1.00
TOTAL	$7.50

9

2D | Consolidation 1

At the deli

Choose the correct sentence (a–h) from the box. Write it in the speech bubble.
Then role-play the conversation.

1 ¹Can I have a cheese sandwich and a chicken sandwich, please?

2 Thank you.

3 Great! Thanks!

5 Here you go.

a) Here you go.	e) How much is that?
✓b) Can I have a cheese sandwich and a chicken sandwich, please?	f) This is your sandwich. This is my sandwich.
c) Thank you.	g) Where's my sandwich?
d) Oh, sorry.	h) $9.25.

Motivator quiz: General knowledge

Circle the correct answer. Check your answers and write your score.

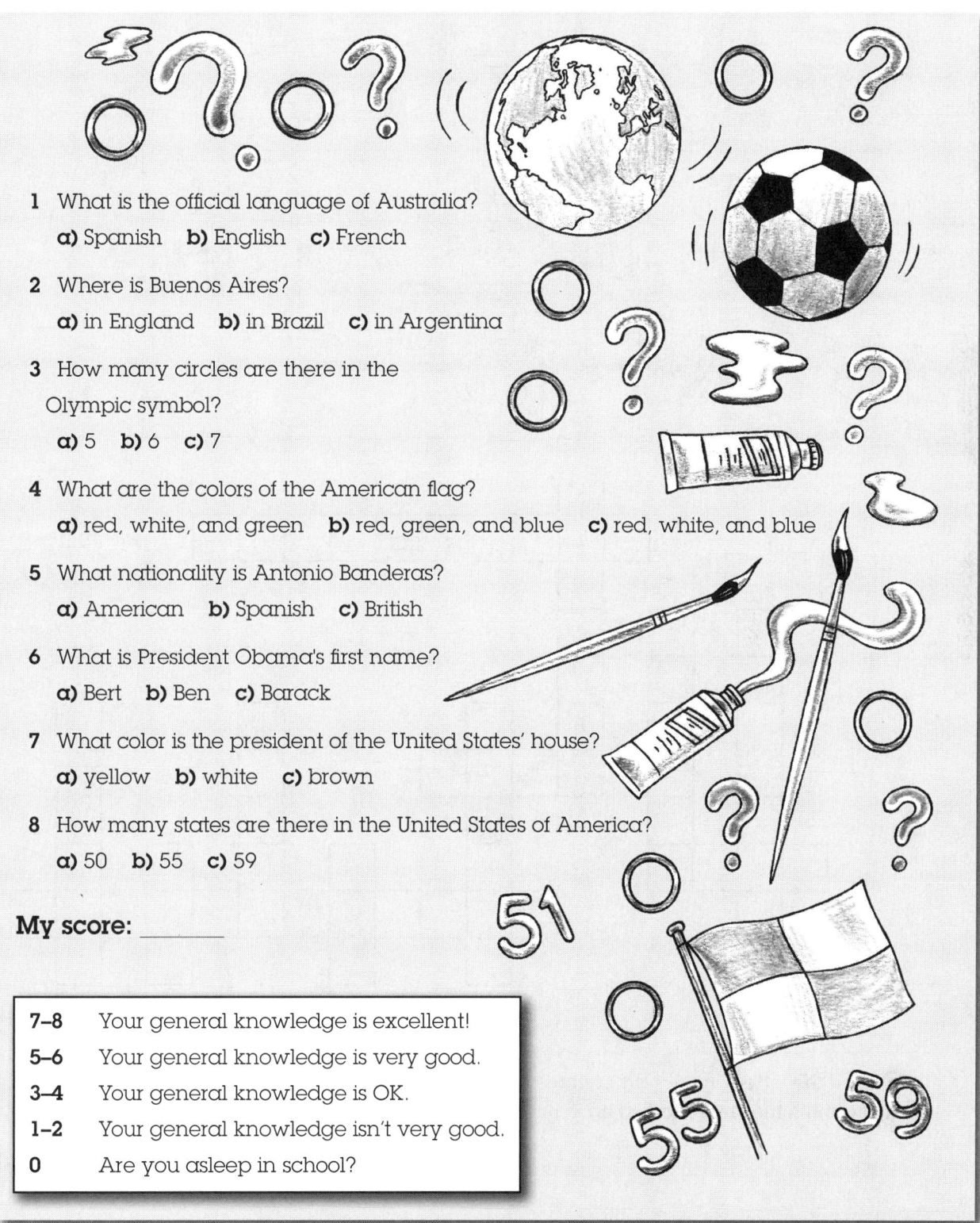

1 What is the official language of Australia?

    a) Spanish   **b)** English   **c)** French

2 Where is Buenos Aires?

    a) in England   **b)** in Brazil   **c)** in Argentina

3 How many circles are there in the
Olympic symbol?

    a) 5   **b)** 6   **c)** 7

4 What are the colors of the American flag?

    a) red, white, and green   **b)** red, green, and blue   **c)** red, white, and blue

5 What nationality is Antonio Banderas?

    a) American   **b)** Spanish   **c)** British

6 What is President Obama's first name?

    a) Bert   **b)** Ben   **c)** Barack

7 What color is the president of the United States' house?

    a) yellow   **b)** white   **c)** brown

8 How many states are there in the United States of America?

    a) 50   **b)** 55   **c)** 59

My score: _____

7–8	Your general knowledge is excellent!
5–6	Your general knowledge is very good.
3–4	Your general knowledge is OK.
1–2	Your general knowledge isn't very good.
0	Are you asleep in school?

1 Find the picture clues and complete the crossword.

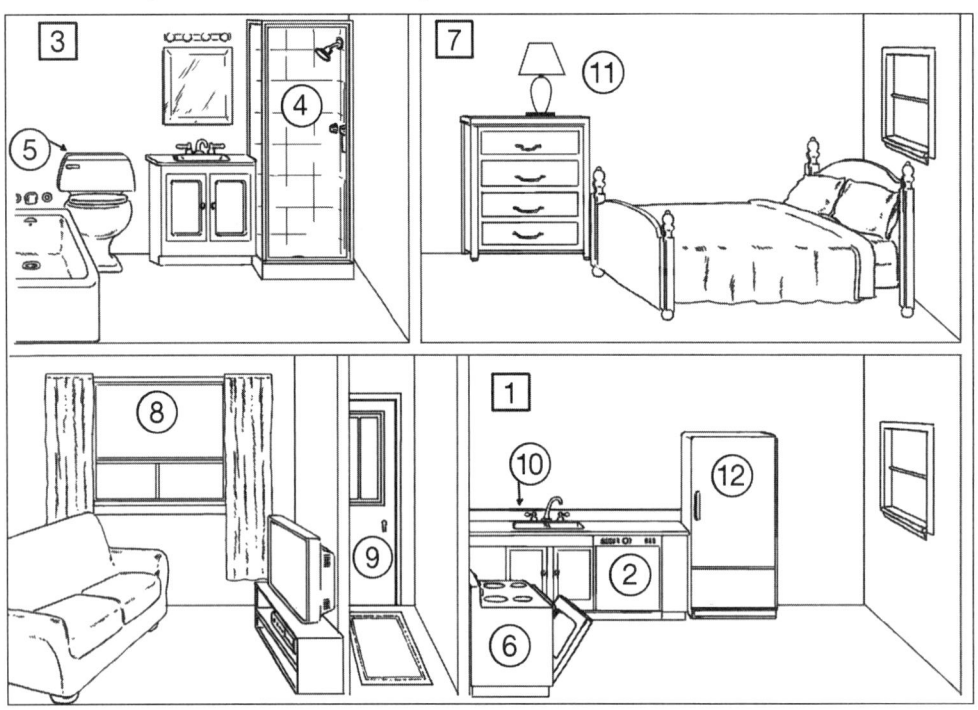

2 Find the letters in the gray squares and write them in the boxes.
Unscramble the letters to find an item for the house.

3B Find the objects

1 Circle 15 things you might find in your home.

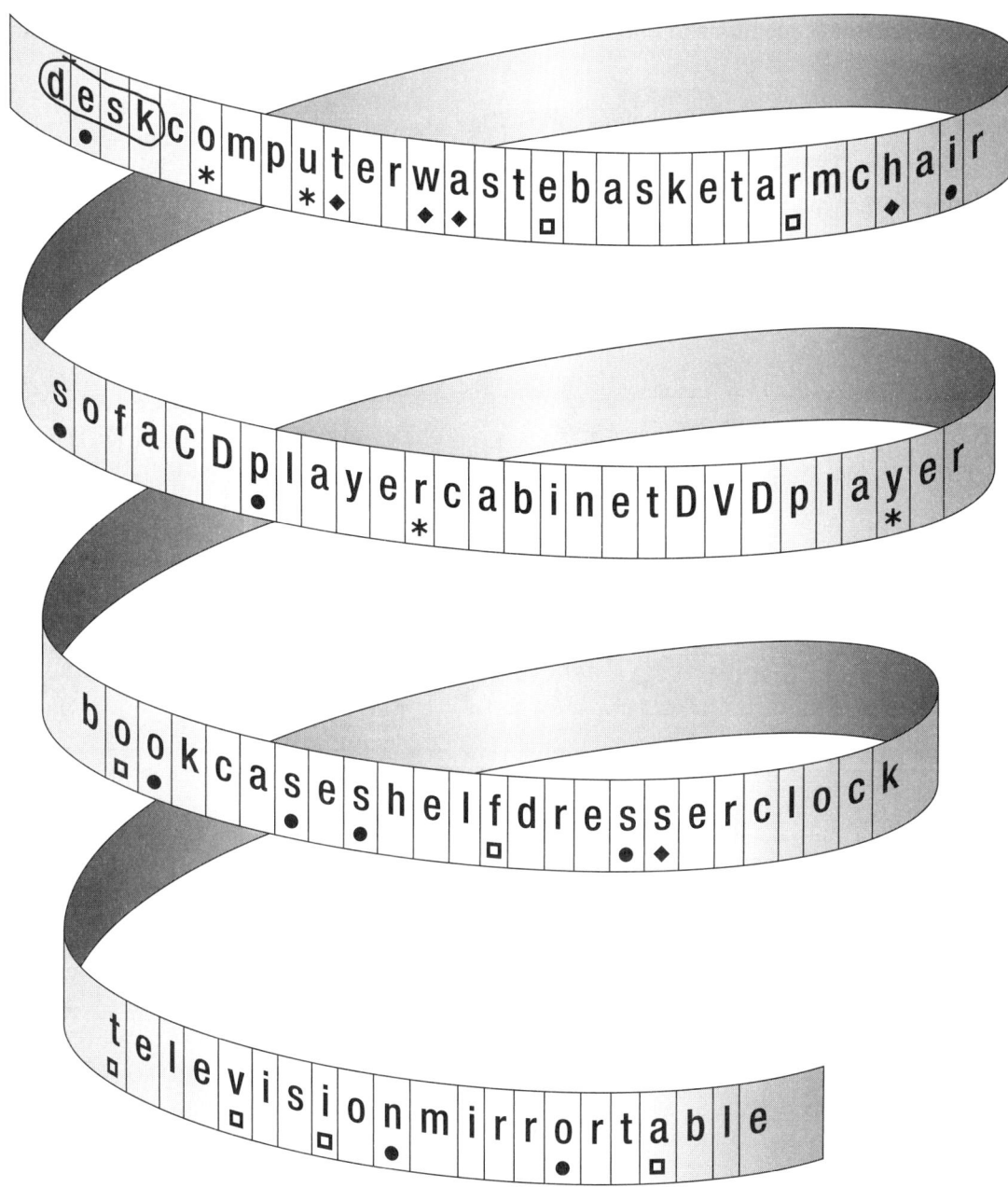

2 Find the letters with symbols. Write them under their symbols.
Unscramble the letters to make words. Answer the question.

◆					*						☐								●						

t	w	h	s	a																					

What's					

Your answer: _____

3c Where are they?

Student A

1 Ask Student B questions to find these people:

Sanjay
Tom
Tina
Kevin

A: Where's Sanjay?   B: He's in front of Emma.

2 Ask questions to find where these objects are in Student B's picture.

A: Where's the bag?   B: It's …

Class 4A Hill Road High School

Tina   Ana   Mark   Emma   Arturo

Marta   Katy   Charlene   Davina

Student B

1 Ask Student A questions to find these people:

Charlene
Arturo
Davina
Ana

A: Where's Charlene?   B: She's next to Katy.

2 Ask questions to find where they are in Student A's picture.

A: Where's the camera?   B: It's …

Class 4A Hill Road High School

Tina   Mark   Tom   Emma

Marta   Kevin   Katy   Sanjay

What's your style?

Compare Picture A and Picture B. Find and write nine differences. Use the words in the text below.

Living Room Magic

There's everything for your living room at Total Home: sofas, armchairs, tables, bookcases, shelves, mirrors, CD players, televisions, lamps.

Picture A

1 *There are two sofas.*

2 *There aren't* _____ .

3 _____ .

4 _____ .

5 _____ .

6 _____ .

7 _____ .

8 _____ .

9 _____ .

Picture B

1 *There aren't any sofas.*

2 _____ .

3 _____ .

4 _____ .

5 _____ .

6 _____ .

7 _____ .

8 _____ .

9 _____ .

Call your phone!

Choose the correct sentence (a–f) from the box. Write it in the speech bubble.
Then role–play the conversation.

1

Oh, no! [1] *Where's my cell phone?*

I don't know. Is it in your bag?

2

2 _____

Borrow a cell phone. Call your phone!

3

That's a good idea!

3 _____
_____

Sure, OK.

4

Four-seven-two, nine-one-eight-seven-five-three-four …

Listen! [4] _____

5

5 _____

It's there!

Wait a minute!

6

6 _____

It's here!

a) No, it isn't.
b) Sorry!
c) No, it's there!
d) Can I borrow your cell phone?
✓e) Where's my cell phone?
f) Your phone is in the room!

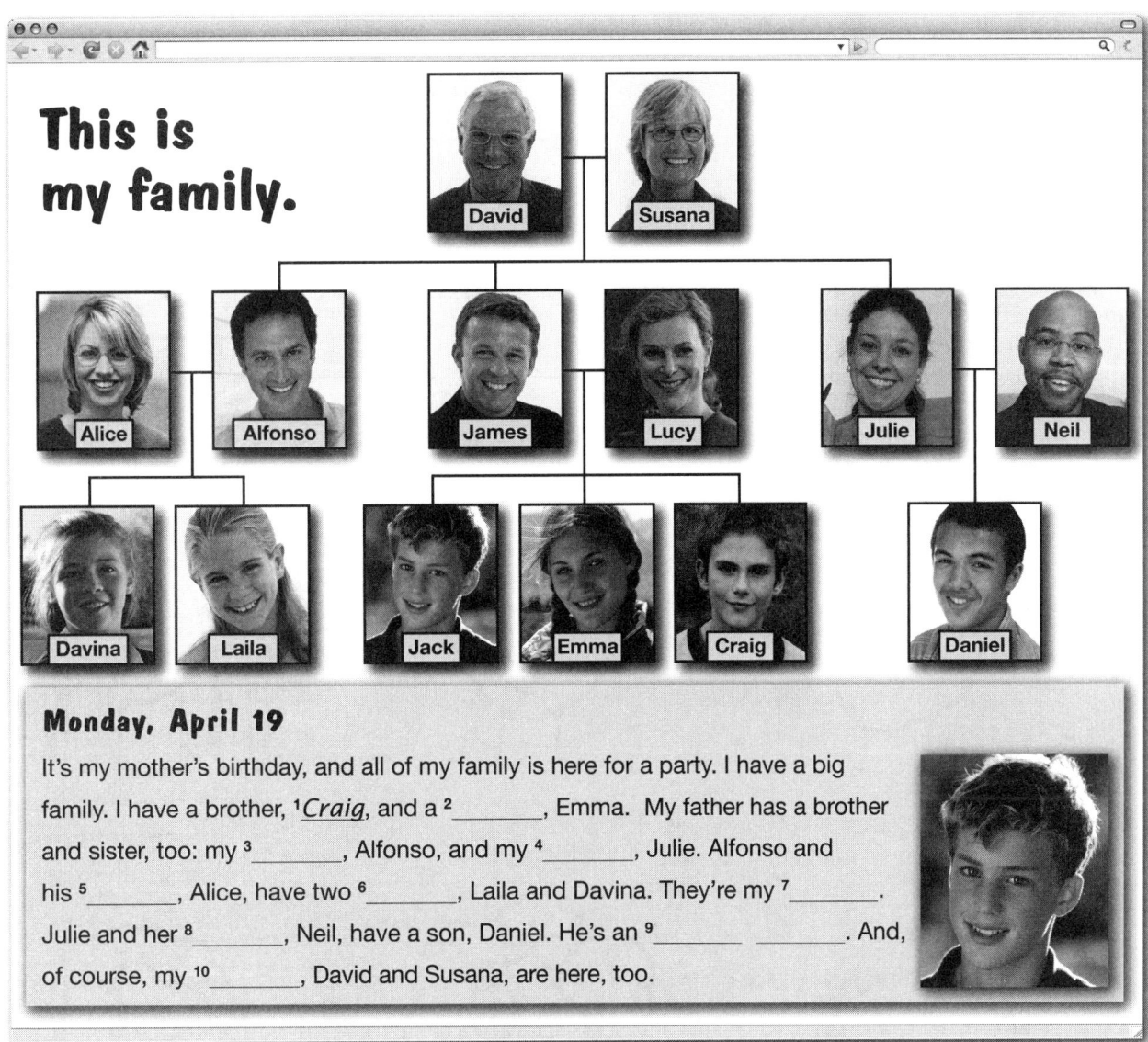

This is my family.

Monday, April 19

It's my mother's birthday, and all of my family is here for a party. I have a big family. I have a brother, ¹*Craig*, and a ²_____, Emma. My father has a brother and sister, too: my ³_____, Alfonso, and my ⁴_____, Julie. Alfonso and his ⁵_____, Alice, have two ⁶_____, Laila and Davina. They're my ⁷_____. Julie and her ⁸_____, Neil, have a son, Daniel. He's an ⁹_____ _____. And, of course, my ¹⁰_____, David and Susana, are here, too.

1 Complete the sentences above about Jack's family.

2 Read the clues and write the words in the grid. Complete the sentence with the mystery word.

1 Craig is Jack's …
2 James is Davina's …
3 Lucy is Jack's …
4 David is Jack's …
5 Emma is Lucy's …
6 Daniel is Alfonso's …
7 James and Lucy are Jack's …

Jack writes a blog.

He is a _____.

4B What do they have?

1 Read the descriptions. Write ✓ for *yes* and ✗ for *no* in the chart.

Tito has short hair and a beard.
Liz, Andrew, and Linda have eyeglasses.
Linda and Andrew have curly hair.
Tito and Jill don't have eyeglasses.
Jill and Linda have long hair.
Oscar has glasses and straight hair.
Liz has short, curly hair.
Tito and Jill have straight hair.
Oscar and Andrew don't have beards.
  They have short hair.

	long hair	straight hair	eyeglasses	beard
Tito	✗			✓
Oscar				
Andrew				
Linda				
Liz				
Jill				

2 Match the information in the chart with the pictures. Write the names.

A _____

B _____

C _____

D _____

E _____

F _____

3 Read what Tito says about his cousin. Complete the last sentence with the name of his cousin.

My cousin has eyeglasses.
My cousin doesn't have straight hair.
My cousin doesn't have short hair.
My cousin's name is _____.

4c Celebrity birthdays

Student A

1 Ask Student B questions and complete the birthday chart with the missing birthdays and letters.

A: When is George Clooney's birthday?
B: It's on May 6.

A: What letter is he?
B: He's I.

Here are the birthdays of twelve celebrities!

George Clooney	I	May 6
Justin Timberlake	A	January 31
Mariah Carey		
Brad Pitt	D	December 18
Avril Lavigne		
Johnny Depp	S	June 9
Lindsay Lohan		
Daniel Radcliffe	N	July 23
Orlando Bloom		
Cameron Diaz	F	August 30
Scarlett Johansson		
Bruce Willis	R	March 19

2 Arrange the birthdays in order (January to December). Look at the chart. Write the letter next to the name to find the mystery celebrity.

1 *Orlando Bloom*   H
2 _____
3 _____
4 _____
5 _____
6 _____
7 _____
8 _____
9 _____
10 _____
11 _____
12 _____

Student B

1 Ask Student A questions and complete the birthday chart with the missing birthdays and letters.

B: When is Justin Timberlake's birthday?
A: It's on January 31.

B: What letter is he?
A: He's A.

Here are the birthdays of twelve celebrities!

George Clooney	I	May 6
Justin Timberlake	A	January 31
Mariah Carey	R	March 27
Brad Pitt		
Avril Lavigne	O	September 27
Johnny Depp		
Lindsay Lohan	O	July 2
Daniel Radcliffe		
Orlando Bloom	H	January 13
Cameron Diaz		
Scarlett Johansson	R	November 22
Bruce Willis		

2 Arrange the birthdays in order (January to December). Look at the chart. Write the letter next to the name to find the mystery celebrity.

1 *Orlando Bloom*   H
2 _____
3 _____
4 _____
5 _____
6 _____
7 _____
8 _____
9 _____
10 _____
11 _____
12 _____

The mystery birthday cake

**Choose the correct sentence (a–e) from the box. Write it in the speech bubble.
Then role-play the conversation.**

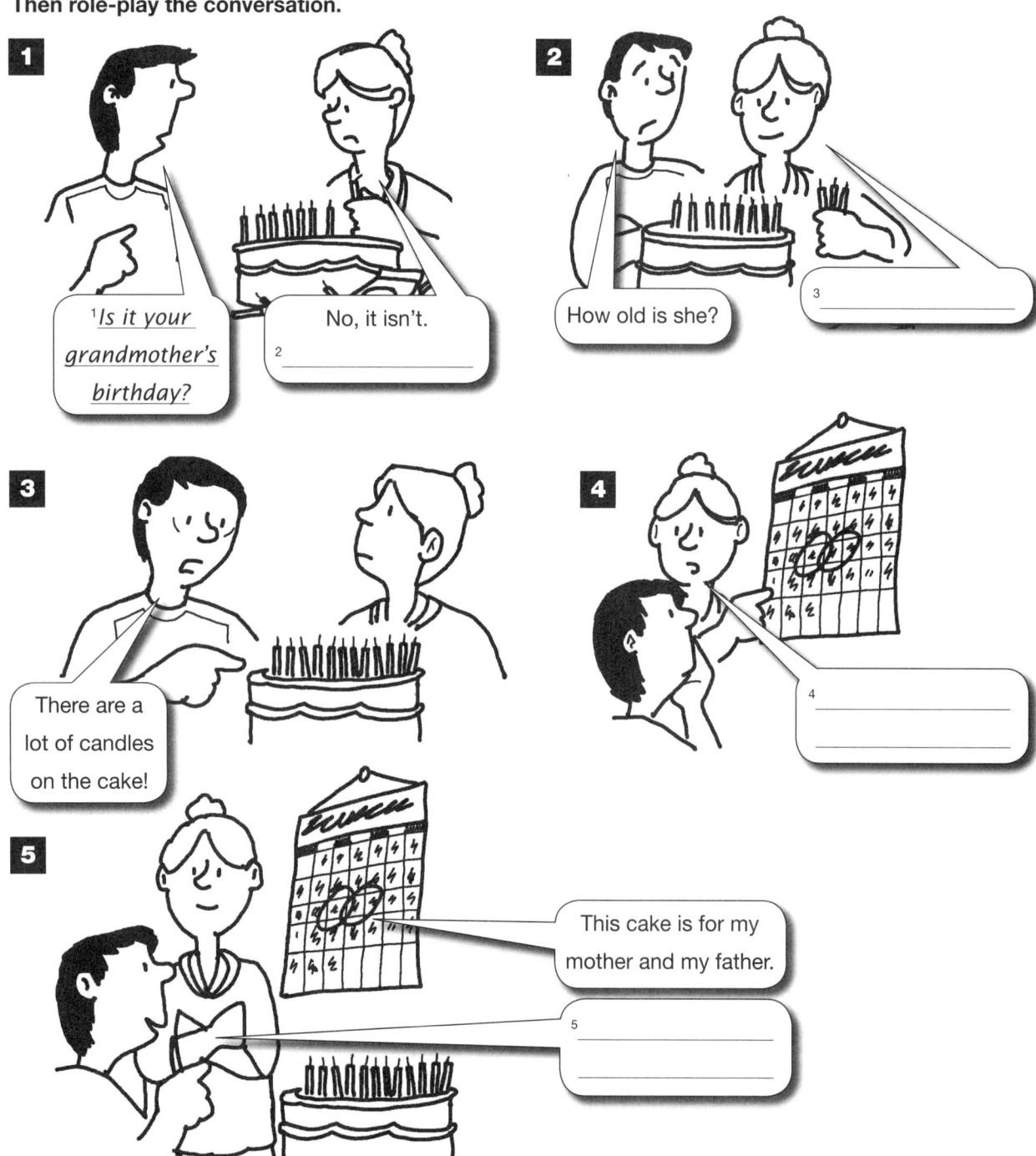

1

¹*Is it your grandmother's birthday?*

No, it isn't.
2 _____

2

How old is she?

3 _____

3

There are a lot of candles on the cake!

4

4 _____

5

This cake is for my mother and my father.

5 _____

a) I understand now! There are 72 candles on the cake.

✓b) Is it your grandmother's birthday?

c) It's my mother's birthday.

d) My father's birthday is tomorrow. He's 37.

e) She's 35.

Motivator quiz: Popular culture

Answer the questions. Check your answers and write your score.

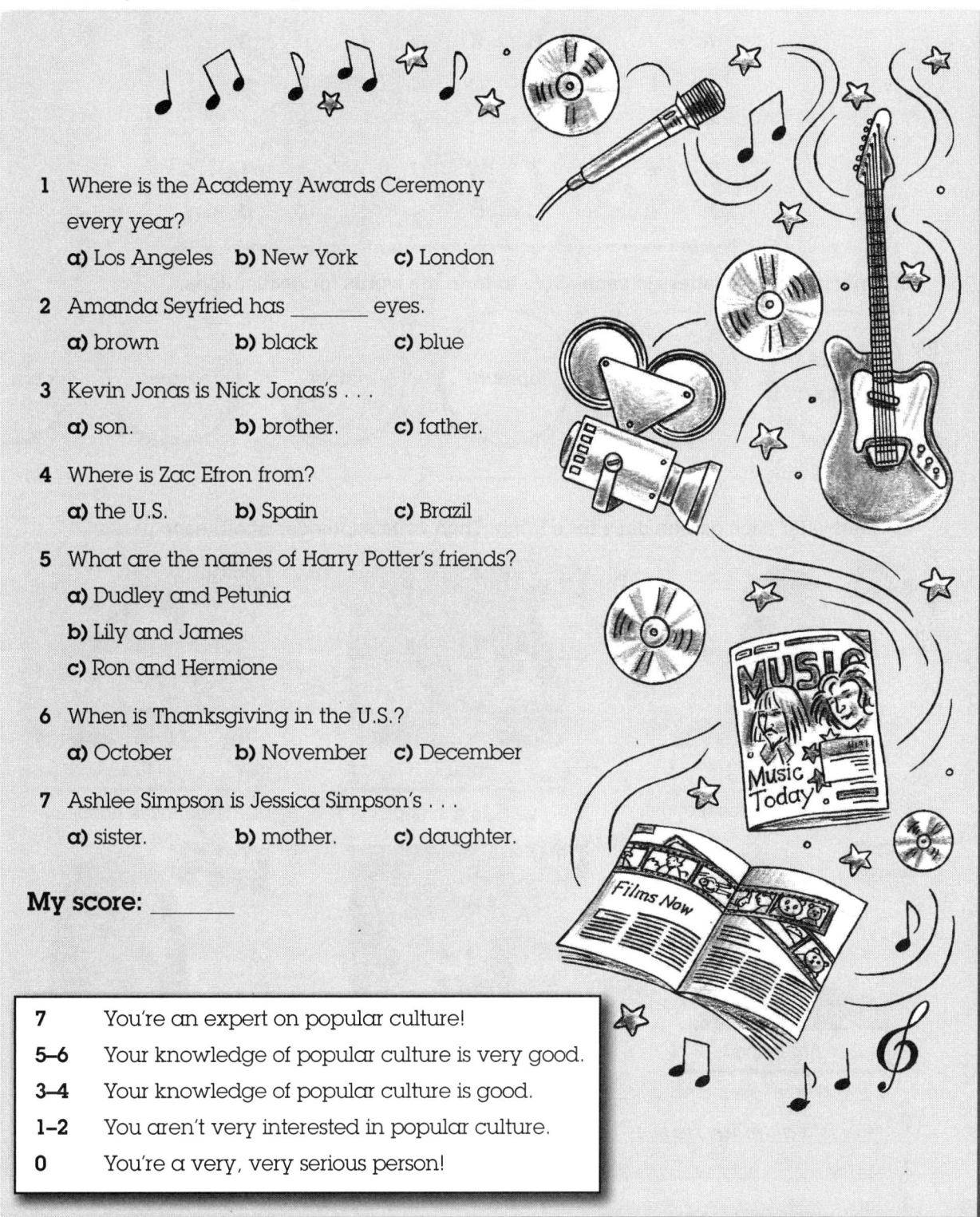

1 Where is the Academy Awards Ceremony every year?
   a) Los Angeles   **b)** New York   **c)** London

2 Amanda Seyfried has _____ eyes.
   a) brown   **b)** black   **c)** blue

3 Kevin Jonas is Nick Jonas's . . .
   a) son.   **b)** brother.   **c)** father.

4 Where is Zac Efron from?
   a) the U.S.   **b)** Spain   **c)** Brazil

5 What are the names of Harry Potter's friends?
   a) Dudley and Petunia
   b) Lily and James
   c) Ron and Hermione

6 When is Thanksgiving in the U.S.?
   a) October   **b)** November   **c)** December

7 Ashlee Simpson is Jessica Simpson's . . .
   a) sister.   **b)** mother.   **c)** daughter.

My score: _____

7	You're an expert on popular culture!
5–6	Your knowledge of popular culture is very good.
3–4	Your knowledge of popular culture is good.
1–2	You aren't very interested in popular culture.
0	You're a very, very serious person!

5A He's a plumber.

1 Find ten jobs in the word search puzzle.

S	E	C	R	E	T	A	R	Y	W
F	B	P	F	A	C	H	E	F	A
W	U	L	A	C	T	O	R	M	I
A	I	U	N	K	Q	L	D	S	T
I	L	M	D	O	C	T	O	R	R
T	D	B	A	R	T	I	S	T	E
E	E	E	Z	W	G	V	J	I	S
R	R	R	N	U	R	S	E	Q	S

2 Unscramble the letters in each circle to form the words for occupations.

1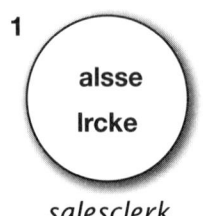
alsse
lrcke

2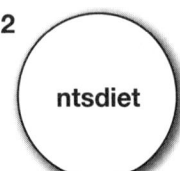
ntsdiet

3
lbpmure

4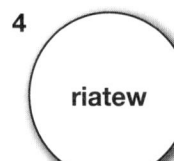
riatew

5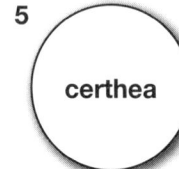
certhea

6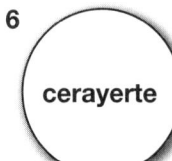
cerayerte

salesclerk _____ _____ _____ _____ _____

3 Read what each person does for a living. Then write sentences about each person.

Max
France

1 I fix kitchens and bathrooms.

Lorna
Brazil

2 I work in a school.

Tony
Italy

3 I work in a hospital.

Andy
Argentina

4 I work in a restaurant.

Gia
America

5 I work in a store at the mall.

Andrea
Mexico

6 I work in an office.

1 *Max is a plumber. He lives in France.*

2 Lorna _____ . _____ .

3 Tony _____ . _____ .

4 Andy _____ . _____ .

5 Gia _____ . _____ .

6 Andrea _____ . _____ .

5B What do they do?

Student A

Use the cues to make questions about the people. Ask Student B the questions and complete the table.

- What … do? • Where … work?
- Where … live? • What languages …?

What does Mario do?

He's an artist.

Name	Job	Place of work	Country	Languages
Mario	*artist*	in a studio	_____	Greek, Italian
Angela	nurse	_____	France	_____
Chen	builder	_____	China	_____
Carl	_____	in a restaurant	_____	Polish, German
Ana	salesclerk	_____	Brazil	_____
Iris	_____	in a kitchen	_____	Spanish, Russian, Japanese

✂ -

Student B

Use the cues to make questions about the people. Ask Student A the questions and complete the chart.

- What … do? • Where … work?
- Where … live? • What languages …?

Where does Mario work?

He works in a factory.

Name	Job	Place of work	Country	Languages
Mario	artist	*in a studio*	Greece	_____
Angela	_____	in a hospital	_____	French, English
Chen	_____	on a construction site	_____	English, Chinese
Carl	waiter	_____	Poland	_____
Ana	_____	at the mall	_____	Portuguese, Spanish
Iris	chef	_____	Argentina	_____

5c *I love it!*

1 Read the opinions of the four people.

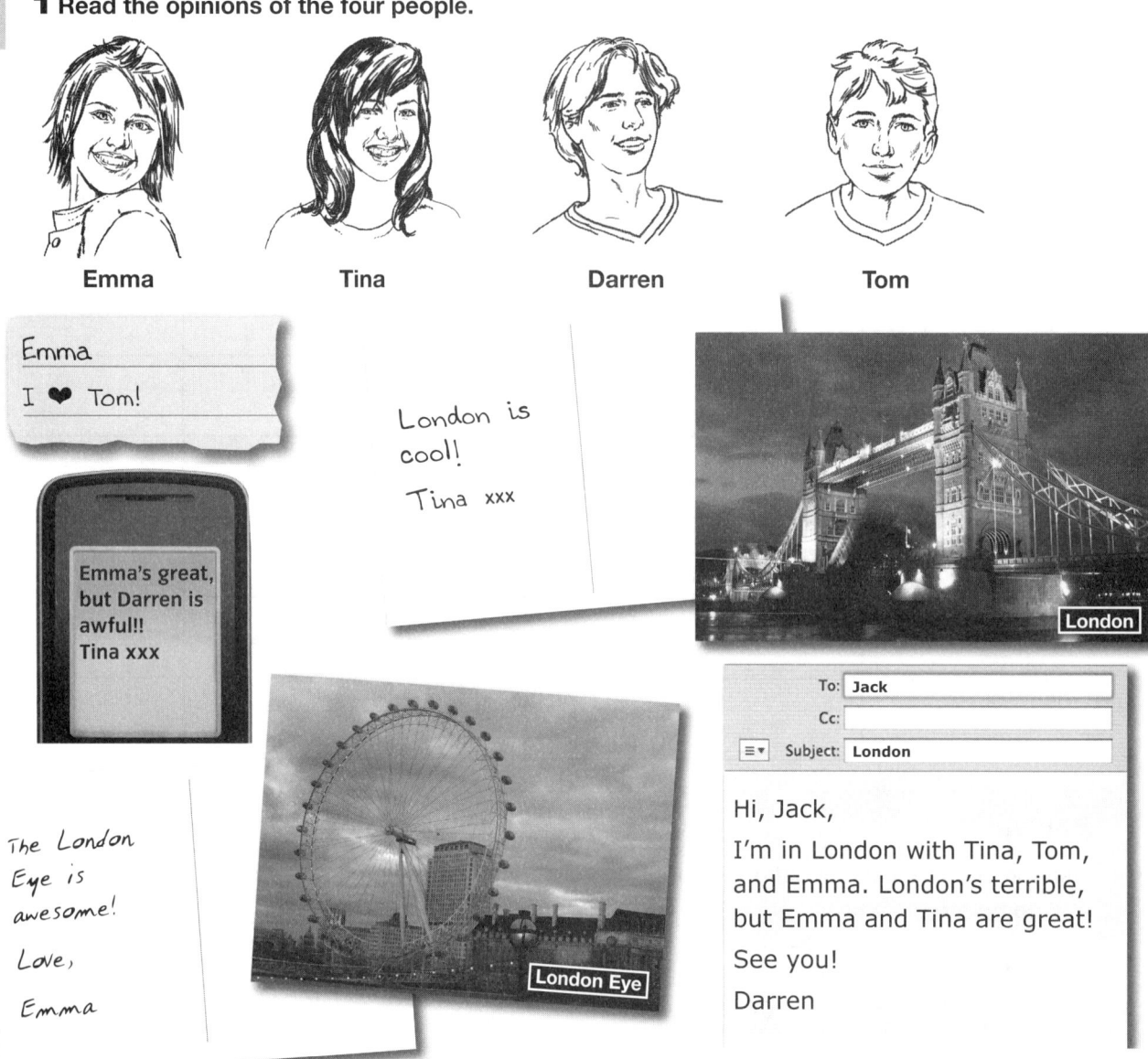

Emma   Tina   Darren   Tom

Emma
I ❤ Tom!

London is
cool!
Tina xxx

Emma's great,
but Darren is
awful!!
Tina xxx

London

The London
Eye is
awesome!
Love,
Emma

London Eye

To:	Jack
Cc:	
☰▾ Subject:	London

Hi, Jack,

I'm in London with Tina, Tom, and Emma. London's terrible, but Emma and Tina are great!

See you!

Darren

2 Look at these pictures. Write sentences using *likes* or *doesn't like* and object pronouns.

1 *She likes him*   .
2 _____ .
3 _____ .
4 _____ .
5 _____ .
6 _____ .
7 _____ .

Who is the mystery guest?

Choose the correct sentence (a–e) from the box. Write it in the speech bubble.
Complete number 6 with the name of the celebrity. Then role-play the conversation.

a) Does he like soccer?
✓b) Is he an actor?
c) Is his wife Spanish, too?

d) Yes, he does. He's from Spain.
e) Yes, he is.

Consolidation 2

My job is great!

1 Cross out the letters for each occupation or job and place of work. Circle the extra letters and write them in the circles.

		Job	Place of work
1	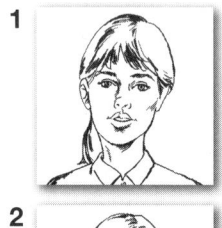	A̶T̶W̶T̶I̶S̶E̶E̶R̶I̶S̶ *waitress*	A̶R̶B̶R̶T̶E̶A̶L̶R̶U̶N̶S̶E̶T̶R̶ *restaurant* (*teiblrer*)
2		D R A C M Z O T A O G _____	S O N I A T H L I P _____ ( )
3		R O S A I Y N E R C G E T _____	C F I O B E R F _____ ( )
4		E R C E T R A E H _____	G H L A S O T C O _____ ( )
5		A S E L S O G K C R L E O _____	D E S O T R _____ ( )

2 Use the extra letters to express each person's opinion of his or her job. Complete the sentences.

1 My job is *terrible*.

2 My job is _____.

3 My job is _____.

4 My job is _____.

5 My job is _____.

A day out

1 Read about the events in Oakland, California, on Saturday. Add the missing times.

> The train ride between San Francisco and Oakland is 15 minutes.
> A football game is usually about three and a half hours (210 minutes).
> The concert is two hours. The movie is 110 minutes.

Moviezone Cinema

Toy Story 3

Starts: 10:20 A.M.   1 _____ P.M.   3:00 P.M.

Ends: 2 _____ P.M.   2:45 P.M.   3 _____ P.M.

Trains from San Francisco to Oakland

Leave	4 _____ A.M.	8:25 A.M.	8:50 A.M.
Arrive	8:20 A.M.	8:40 A.M.	5 _____ A.M.

Trains from Oakland to San Francisco

Leave	7:10 P.M.	6 _____ P.M.	7:50 P.M.
Arrive	7 _____ P.M.	7:45 P.M.	8:05 P.M.

Mike Donald's Hamburgers

Two Angus Burgers for the price of one!
Monday to Saturday
11:45 P.M. – 12:30 P.M.

Oakland Coliseum

Oakland Raiders vs San Francisco 49ers
Starts   3:00 P.M.
Ends   8 ___ P.M.

ABZ Boys

In Concert

at Snow Park
9 _____ P.M. to 2:45 P.M.

OAKLAND MUSEUM

Special exhibition
Treasures from Turkey
10:00 A.M. to 8:00 P.M.

2 Matt and Julio live in San Francisco, California. Work out a schedule for their day in Oakland. Number the events in order and write the times.

> Time in the museum: 60 minutes
> Time for lunch: 45 minutes
> Time between places: 15 minutes minimum

Event	Time
___ Football game at the Oakland Coliseum	_____
___ Movie at Moviezone	_____
___ Exhibition at the Oakland Museum	_____
_1_ Train to Oakland	_8:25 – 8:40_

Event	Time
___ Train to San Francisco	_____
___ Lunch at Mike Donald's	_____
___ Concert at Snow Park	_____

6B One boy's day

Read about this boy's day. Follow the line and choose the correct times for each
activity. Circle the letter next to each correct time and find the boy's name.

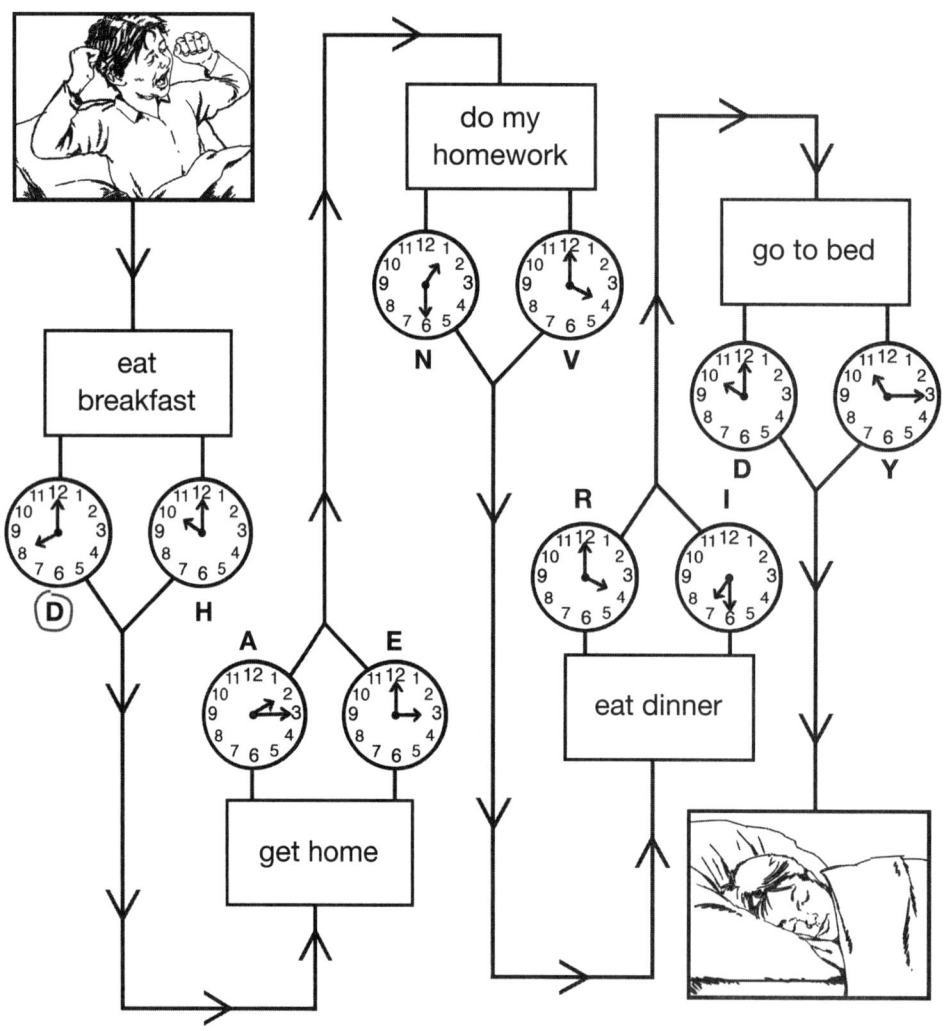

eat breakfast

do my homework

go to bed

N   V

D   Y

R   I

get home

eat dinner

I get up at 7:30 every morning, I eat breakfast,
and I go to school at 8:00. I go home at 2:00,
and I eat lunch at 2:15. In the afternoon I play
video games, and at 4:00 I do my homework.
At night I watch TV, and I call my friends. I eat
dinner at 7:30. I go to bed, and I go to sleep
at 10:00.

His name's

_____ .

At the gym

Read the clues and name the people.

Rosa goes to the gym once a week. She always goes to the gym on Monday.

Tito goes to the gym three times a week.

Rafa goes to the gym three times a week. He never goes on Friday.

Joe goes to the gym twice a week. He never goes on Monday.

Alice never goes to the gym.

Naomi sometimes goes to the gym on Wednesday, but she usually goes on Friday.

Carol always goes to the gym on Monday and Friday.

Carlos goes to the gym once a month. He never goes on Monday or Friday.

1 _____Tito_____   2 _____   3 _____   4 _____

5 _____   6 _____   7 _____   8 _____

A word game

Student A

1 Say numbers and letters to Student B. Write the words in the *Your words* chart.

2 Listen to Student B. Say words from the *Student B's words* chart.

A: B3   B: C4
B: That's *get*.   A: That's *in bed*.

Your words	1	2	3	4
A				
B			*get*	
C				
D				

Student B's words	1	2	3	4
A	go	breakfast	to school	a friend
B	call	get	play	lunch
C	eat	read	to bed	in bed
D	dinner	up	video games	to sleep

3 Make phrases for daily routines with your words. You have one minute! | eat | breakfast | lunch |

✂ -

Student B

1 Listen to Student A. Say words from the *Student A's words* chart.

2 Say numbers and letters to Student A. Write the words in the *Your words* chart.

A: B3   B: C4
B: That's *wake*.   A: That's *in bed*.

Your words	1	2	3	4
A				
B				
C				*in bed*
D				

Student A's words	1	2	3	4
A	video games	to sleep	to bed	in bed
B	play	lunch	get	call
C	read	eat	to school	a friend
D	breakfast	go	up	dinner

3 Make phrases for daily routines with your words. You have one minute! | eat | breakfast | lunch |

Are they identical?

What's the difference between Tim and Tony?
Tony does everything _____ after Tim.

1 Fill in the blanks with the correct verb from the box. Write them in the speech bubbles. Then role-play the conversation. Answer this question about Tim and Tony.

a) eats breakfast	✓c) get up	e) brush my teeth
b) eat breakfast	d) gets up	f) brushes his teeth

We're at home with Tim and Tony. They're twins, and they're identical!

1

We aren't identical. I ¹*get up* at seven o'clock. He ² _____ at seven thirty.

2

I ³ _____ at seven forty-five. ⁴He _____ at eight fifteen.

3

I ⁵ _____ at eight o'clock. He ⁶ _____ _____ at eight thirty.

4

We're very different!

2 Look at the information about Tim. Write about Tony.

1 Tim check his e-mail at six fifty-five. *Tony checks his e-mail at seven twenty-five.*

2 Tim listens to music at four fifteen. _____

3 Tim calls his friends at six o'clock. _____

4 Tim goes to bed at ten fifty. _____

What can you do?

1 Complete the crossword with verbs.

Across

2 _____

3 _____

5 _____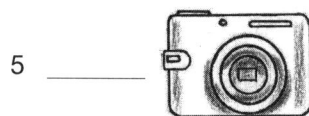

6 _____ a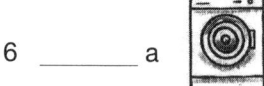

Down

1 _____ a

3 _____ a

4 _____ on a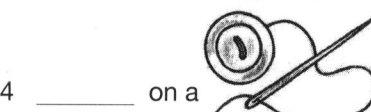

2 Make sentences about yourself, your family, and your friends. Use the verbs in the crossword.

Example: *My brother can use a computer very well.*

1 _____
2 _____  can _____  very well.

3 _____
4 _____  can _____,  but not very well.

5 _____
6 _____  can't _____.

An accident in the kitchen

Look at the pictures. Find ten differences. Use the words in the box.

• banana(s) • onion(s) • cheese • carrot(s) • egg(s) • butter • milk • pasta • bread • meat

Picture A

1 *There are some bananas.*

2 *There are two onions.*

3 _____.

4 _____.

5 _____.

6 _____.

7 _____.

8 _____.

9 _____.

10 _____.

Picture B

1 *There aren't any bananas.*

2 *There are three onions.*

3 _____.

4 _____.

5 _____.

6 _____.

7 _____.

8 _____.

9 _____.

10 _____.

Where am I?

Student A

1 Match the places with the pictures.

1 bookstore
2 coffee shop
3 drugstore
4 train station

5 supermarket
6 health club
7 post office

2 What places from Exercise 1 are missing on the map? Ask Student B questions about them. Draw the places on the map.

> • next to   • in   • across from
> • behind   • in front of   • near
> • between   • on the corner of

A: Excuse me, is there a bookstore near here?

B: Yes, there's one on the corner of Farm Road and High Street.

A: Thanks very much.

Student B

1 Match the places with the pictures.

1 bookstore
2 coffee shop
3 drugstore
4 train station

5 supermarket
6 health club
7 post office

2 What places from Exercise 1 are missing on the map? Ask Student A questions about them. Draw the places on the map.

> • next to   • in   • across from
> • behind   • in front of   • near
> • between   • on the corner of

B: Excuse me, is there a train station near here?

A: Yes, there's one on High Street. It's across from the park.

B: Thanks very much.

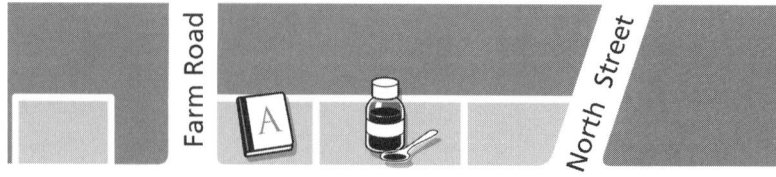

Motivator quiz: Food

Answer the questions. Check your answers and write your score.

1 Where is pizza from?

   a) Greece **b)** Italy **c)** France

2 Which of these is not a healthy food?

   a) honey **b)** carrots **c)** cookies

3 Which of these is in pasta?

   a) sugar **b)** bananas **c)** eggs

4 Which of these is sometimes called a fruit?

   a) potato **b)** carrot **c)** tomato

5 Which of these is not a dairy product?

   a) butter **b)** honey **c)** cheese

6 Which of these foods do vegetarians eat?

   a) meat **b)** chicken **c)** pasta

7 Which of these is not in an omelette?

   a) rice **b)** salt **c)** eggs

8 Which of these is not an ingredient of pizza?

   a) apple **b)** onion **c)** tomato

My score: _____

7–8	Food is your favorite subject!
5–6	You know a lot about food.
3–4	You know a little about food.
1–2	You aren't very interested in food.
0	Maybe you don't like food at all!

Categories

Cross out the letters for the word in each picture. Write the word in the correct category below. Make an extra word for the same category with the extra letters.

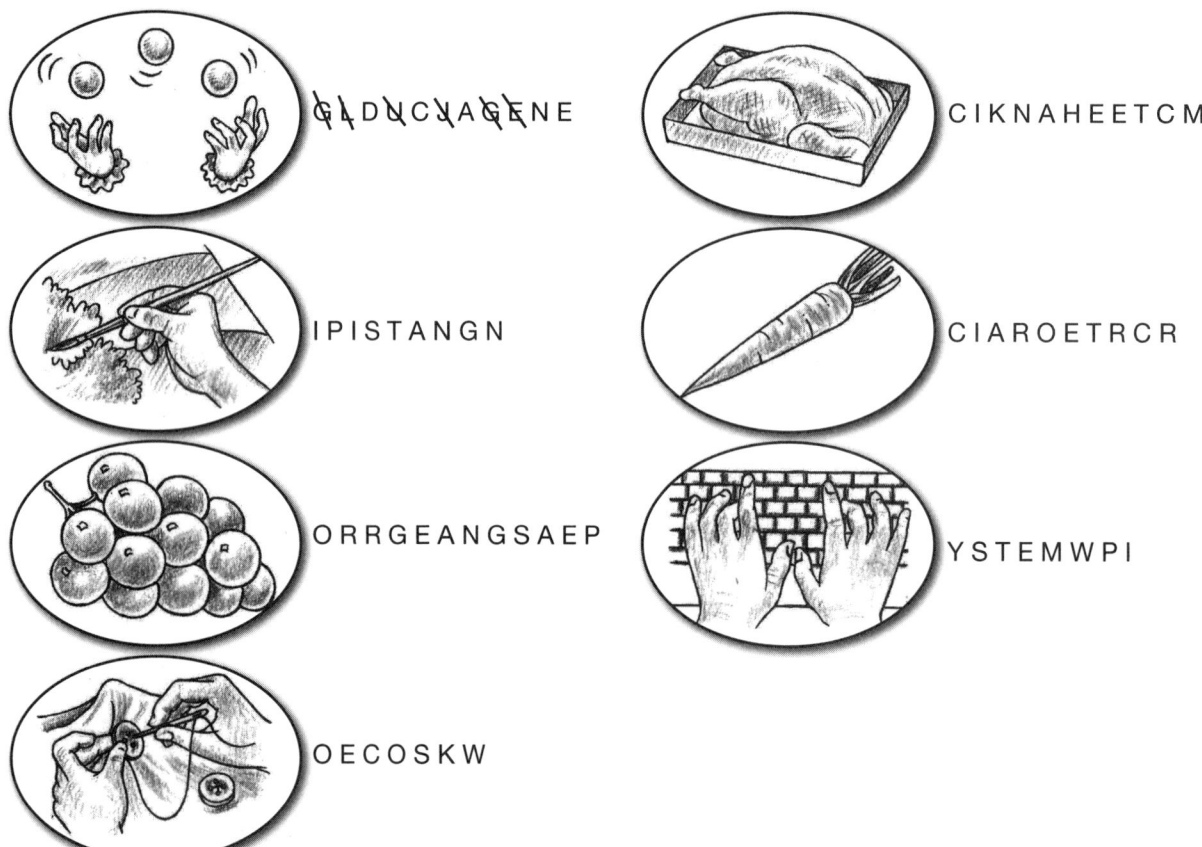

GↃDↃCↃAGↃENE

CIKNAHEETCM

IPISTANGN

CIAROETRCR

ORRGEANGSAEP

YSTEMWPI

OECOSKW

	Picture word	Extra word
Abilities	*juggle*	*dance*
Food		

8A What's the weather like?

Student A

Ask Student B questions about the weather. Write the details on the weather map.

A: What's the weather like in Sydney?
B: It's raining and it's warm.

A: What's the temperature?
B: It's 68 degrees.

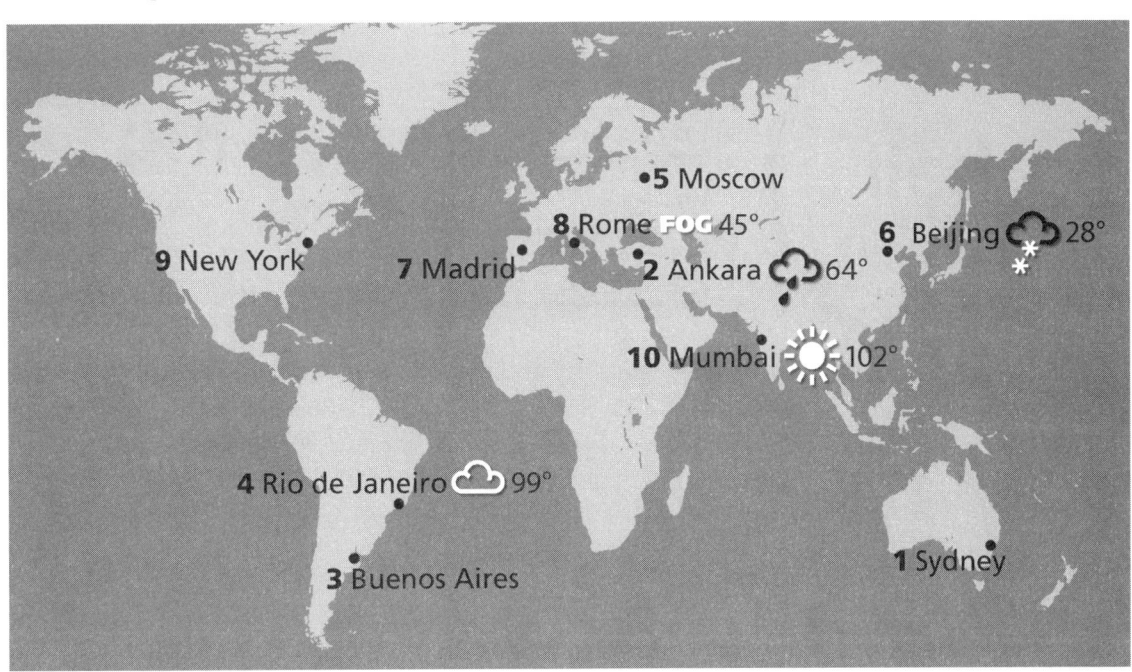

- **5** Moscow
- **8** Rome FOG 45°
- **9** New York
- **7** Madrid
- **2** Ankara 64°
- **6** Beijing 28°
- **10** Mumbai 102°
- **4** Rio de Janeiro 99°
- **3** Buenos Aires
- **1** Sydney

✂ -

Student B

Ask Student A questions about the weather. Write the details on the weather map.

B: What's the weather like in Ankara?
A: It's raining and it's warm.

B: What's the temperature?
A: It's 64 degrees.

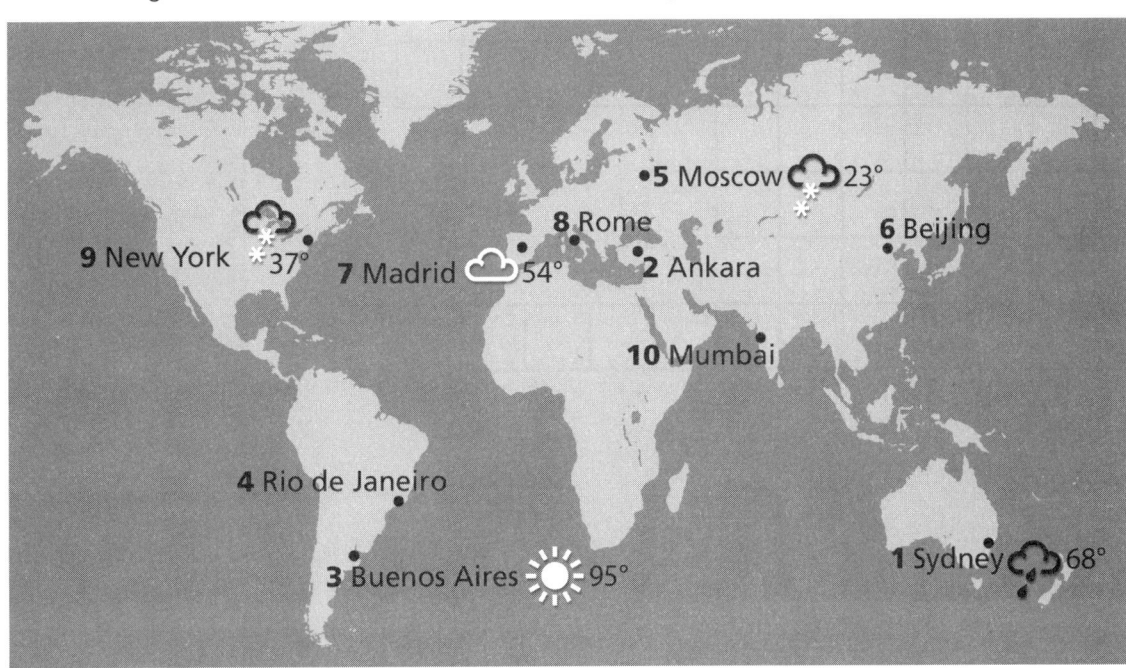

- **5** Moscow 23°
- **8** Rome
- **9** New York 37°
- **7** Madrid 54°
- **2** Ankara
- **6** Beijing
- **10** Mumbai
- **4** Rio de Janeiro
- **3** Buenos Aires 95°
- **1** Sydney 68°

37

8B Mixed-up sports

1 Unscramble the sports words. Write the words in the grid in Exercise 2.

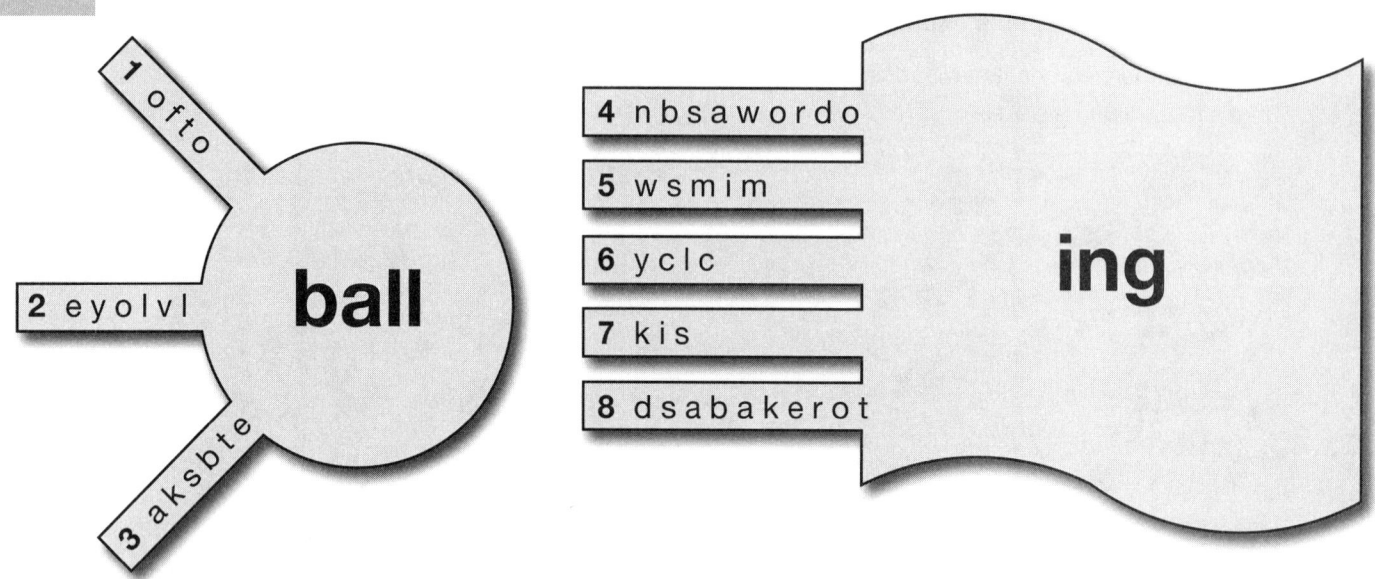

1 o f t o

2 e y o l v l

3 a k s b t e

ball

4 n b s a w o r d o

5 w s m i m

6 y c l c

7 k i s

8 d s a b a k e r o t

ing

2 Unscramble the letters in the gray squares to make two more sports. Add them to the descriptions of the sports stars.

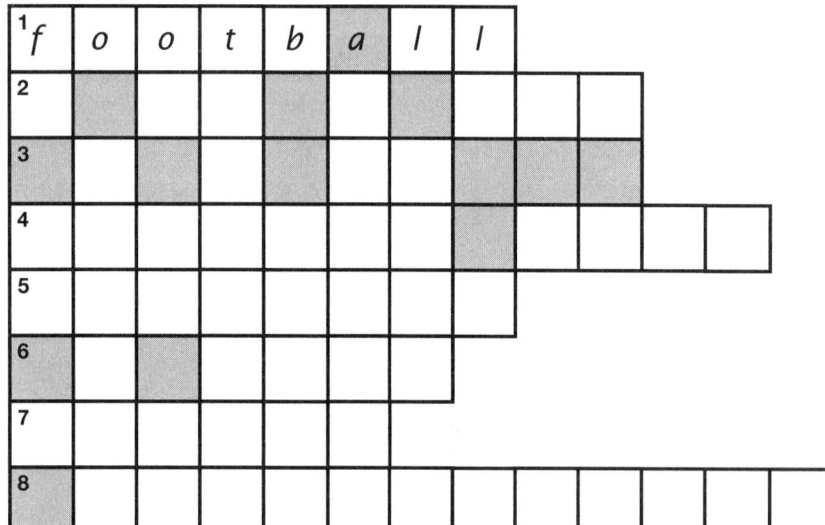

¹f	o	o	t	b	a	l	l

a David Beckham

English _____ player

b Alex Rodriguez

American _____ player

Homebody or party animal?

1 Read about Jason's free time and complete the quiz for him.

Jason Morales is a radio DJ. This is what he says about his free time.

> **❝** My radio show starts at 6 o'clock in the morning, so I don't like going to parties on weeknights. I prefer watching TV at home. I have a computer, and I sometimes surf the Internet, but I prefer chatting with friends online.
>
> On Saturday nights I don't stay home and watch DVDs. I prefer going to the movies. What about Sundays? I like sports, but a lot of my friends play tennis on Sunday morning – and I hate it! I prefer skateboarding. On Sunday afternoon in the summer I sometimes have a barbecue, but my favorite thing is to sit outside and listen to music.
>
> Cycling is OK in the summer, but if it's hot my favorite activity is going to the beach with my friends. **❞**

Are you an introvert or an extrovert?

Try our quiz and find out.

Which do you prefer?		Jason prefers . . .	I prefer . . .
On weeknights	a) going to parties b) watching TV	b)	
	a) chatting with friends online b) surfing the Internet		
On Saturday nights	a) going to the movies b) watching DVDs		
On Sunday morning	a) playing tennis b) skateboarding		
On Sunday afternoon	a) having a barbeque b) sitting outside and listening to music		
In the summer	a) going to the beach with my friends b) cycling		

Key
Mostly (a): You're an extrovert. You like being with lots of people.
Equal (a) and (b): You're a balance of extrovert and introvert. You like being with groups of people, but you like your own company, too.
Mostly (b): You're an introvert. You prefer to be with one or two friends and you're happy on your own.

2 Complete the quiz for yourself. Then tell the class about you and Jason.

On weekday nights Jason prefers . . ., but I prefer . . .

Motivator quiz: Sports

Answer the questions. Check your answers and write your score.

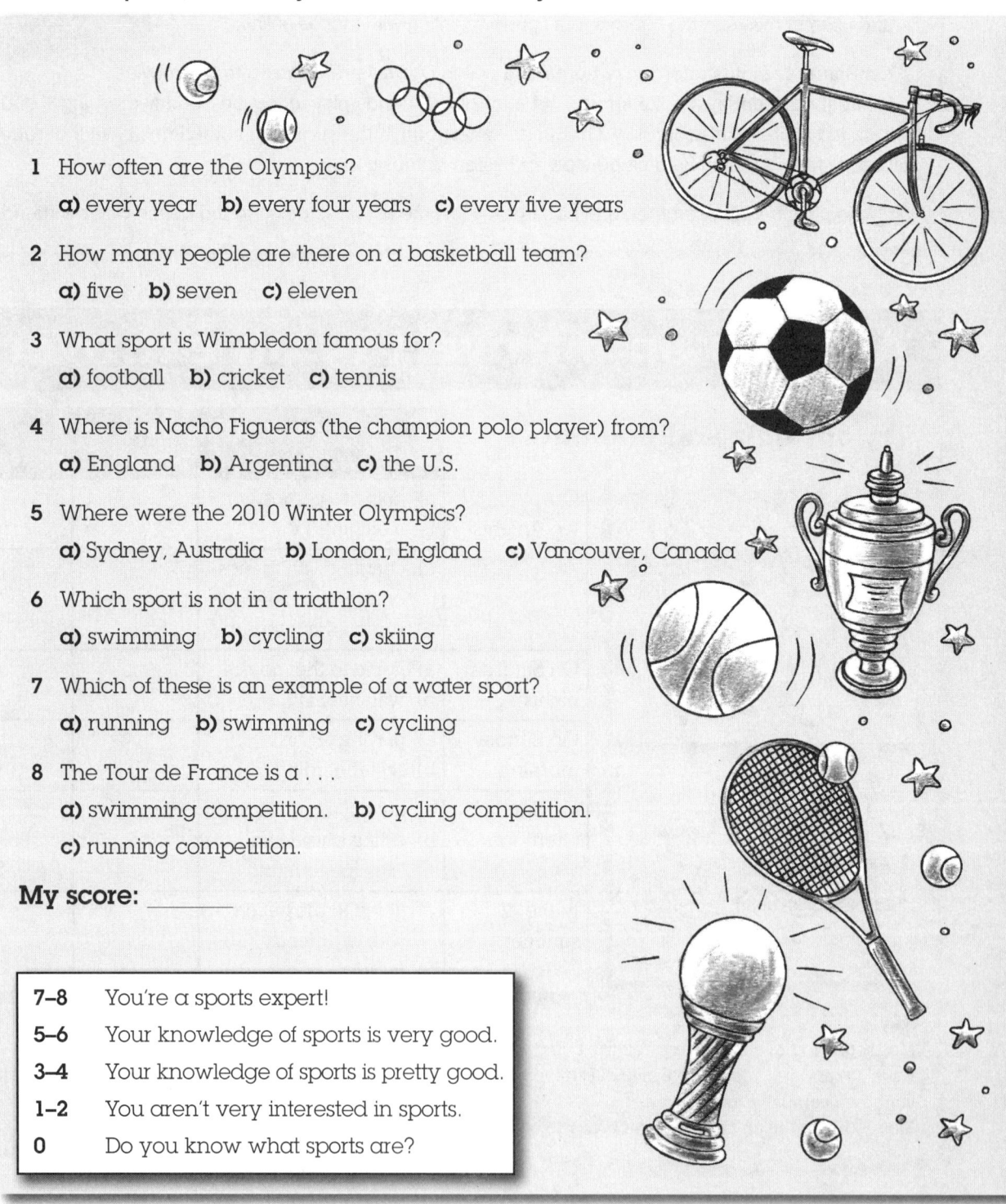

1 How often are the Olympics?

   a) every year   **b)** every four years   **c)** every five years

2 How many people are there on a basketball team?

   a) five   **b)** seven   **c)** eleven

3 What sport is Wimbledon famous for?

   a) football   **b)** cricket   **c)** tennis

4 Where is Nacho Figueras (the champion polo player) from?

   a) England   **b)** Argentina   **c)** the U.S.

5 Where were the 2010 Winter Olympics?

   a) Sydney, Australia   **b)** London, England   **c)** Vancouver, Canada

6 Which sport is not in a triathlon?

   a) swimming   **b)** cycling   **c)** skiing

7 Which of these is an example of a water sport?

   a) running   **b)** swimming   **c)** cycling

8 The Tour de France is a . . .

   a) swimming competition.   **b)** cycling competition.

   c) running competition.

My score: _____

7–8	You're a sports expert!
5–6	Your knowledge of sports is very good.
3–4	Your knowledge of sports is pretty good.
1–2	You aren't very interested in sports.
0	Do you know what sports are?

I ✘ text messages

Choose the correct phrase from the box (a–g). Write it in the speech bubble.
Then role–play the conversation.

1 ¹*Why don't we* go shopping?

No, ² _____.

2 ³ _____ to the beach.

I'm not sure.

3 ⁴ _____ staying at home?

OK. ⁵ _____.

4 I don't understand. ⁶ _____ hanging out with our friends.

5 Yes, I do.

6 462 Mail Box Full

But ⁷ _____ I don't have time to read them!

a) That's a good idea	c) You love	e) I have 462 text messages	✓f) Why don't we
b) Let's go	d) How about	on my phone!	g) not today

9A Who was the robber?

1 Read about the robbery. Find out where each person was at 4:40. Draw a circle for each person on the plan of the house. Write the first names in the circles.

Famous painting stolen

At 4:30 on Sunday this famous painting was in the dining room of Morton House, the home of Russian millionaire Alex Popov. But at 4:45 it wasn't there . . .

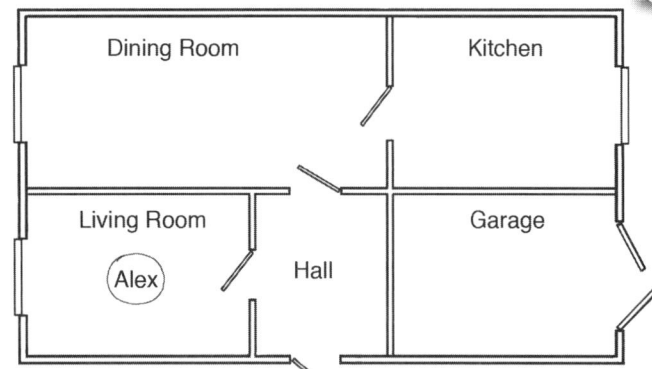

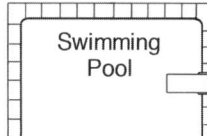

Alex Popov –
millionaire art collector

I was in the dining room at 4:30. Then I was in the living room with my mother.

Ian Grubber –
Mr. Popov's friend

I was in the swimming pool. Mrs. Popov and Mrs. Cole were in the kitchen.

James Cole –
Mr. Popov's driver

I was in the garage. I was with Jimmy.

Ana Popov –
Mr. Popov's mother

I was in the living room. My son was with me.

Janice Cole – the
cook at Money House

I was with Mrs. Popov. My husband wasn't with me.

Natasha Popov –
Mr. Popov's wife

I was in the kitchen with Mrs. Cole. Mr. Grubber was in the swimming pool.

Lenny Rock –
the security guard

I was in front of the house all the time.

Jimmy Cole –
James Cole's son

I was with my father.

2 Answer the questions.

1 Who do you think is the robber? _____

2 Why do you think that? _____

9B *Where did they meet?*

Student A

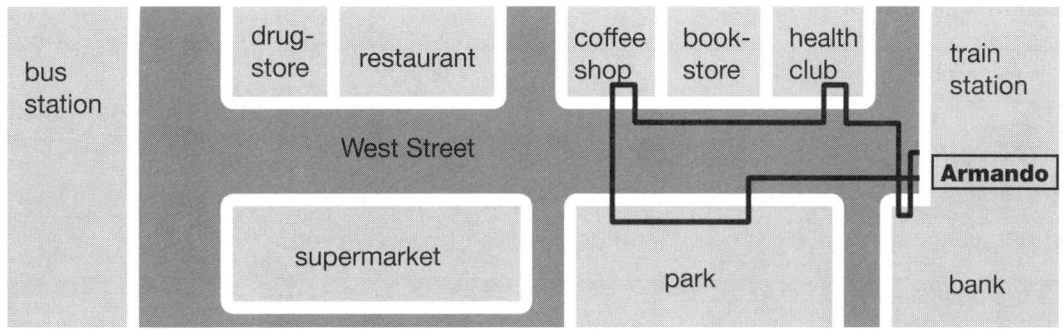

1 Look at the map of Armando's route and complete the text with the correct prepositions from the box.

> across   along   past   into   out of

2 Tell Student B Armando's route. Use the text.

3 Now listen to Student B and complete the map with Monica's route.

4 Answer the question.

Where did Armando talk to Monica? _____

At eleven o'clock Armando walked ¹*out of* the train station. He walked ² _____ the bank, then he walked ³ _____ West Street. He walked ⁴ _____ the health club. At one thirty he walked ⁵ _____ the health club. He walked ⁶ _____ the bookstore and ⁷ _____ the coffee shop. At two o'clock he walked ⁸ _____ the coffee shop. He walked ⁹ _____ West Street and ¹⁰ _____ the park. Then he walked ¹¹ _____ the park and ¹² _____ West Street to the bus station.

- -

Student B

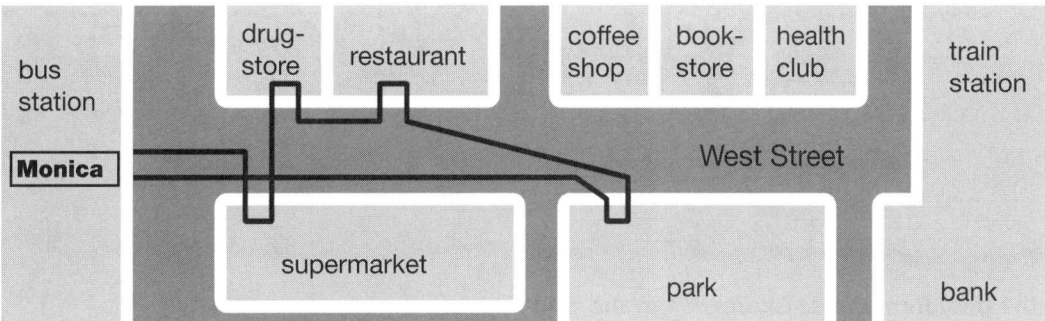

1 Look at the map of Monica's route and complete the text with the correct prepositions from the box.

> across   along   past   into   out of

2 Listen to Student A and complete the map with Armando's route.

3 Tell Student A Monica's route. Use the text.

4 Answer the question.

Where did Monica talk to Armando? _____

At twelve o'clock Monica walked ¹*out of* the bus station. She walked ² _____ the supermarket. Then she walked ³ _____ West Street and ⁴ _____ the drugstore. At one o'clock she walked ⁵ _____ the drugstore and ⁶ _____ the restaurant. At two o'clock she walked ⁷ _____ the restaurant. She walked ⁸ _____ West Street and ⁹ _____ the park. Then she walked ¹⁰ _____ the park and ¹¹ _____ West Street. She walked ¹² _____ the supermarket to the bus station.

9c How are you?

1 Complete the text messages with the past form of the verbs in the box.
Match each message with a picture.

| • shout • remember • practice • call • miss • finish • ~~watch~~ |

Your text messages

Text us! Tell us how you are right now! Send us a photo of yourself, too.

1 I _watched_ a TV program about wild animals in danger, and now I'm sad.

2 I'm angry with my friend. He _____ at me this morning.

3 I'm tired. I _____ the piano for three hours today.

4 I was bored, but then I _____ there's a great concert in the park tonight.

5 I'm happy! I _____ my exams today!

6 I'm upset. I _____ my friend's birthday party because I was sick.

7 My friend _____ me. We talked about our vacation plans. I'm excited.

A 7

B

C

D

E

F

G

2 Write the past forms from Exercise 1 in the grid and find the mystery adjective.

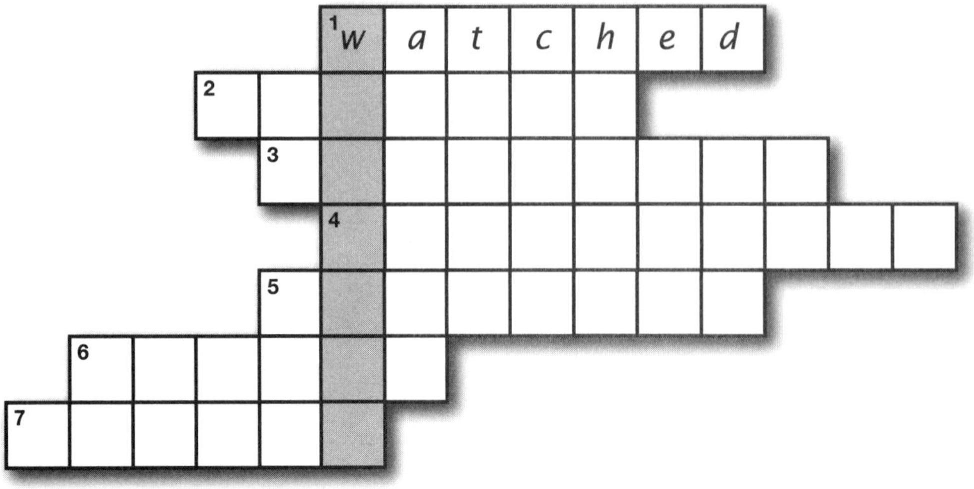

		¹w	a	t	c	h	e	d		
2										
	3									
	4									
	5									
6										
7										

I know the answer!

Choose the correct sentence from the box. Write it in the speech bubble. Then role-play the conversation.

1

What's the matter, Leo? Why are you worried?

¹*There was a geography test at school.*

2

There were ten questions.
2 _____

Oh, no.

3

But I know my answer was right! So I scored one point.

Really? ³ _____

4

What's the capital of the U.S.?

4 _____

5

5 _____

But Leo . . .

6

6 _____

TEST
%10

Oh, no!

a) What did you say?	✓d) There was a geography test at school.
b) I only answered one question.	e) The capital of the U.S. is Washington, D.C.
c) New York, of course.	f) What was the question?

Construct a story!

1 Choose one phrase from each row and make a story.

1	Last night he	Last night my brother	Tomorrow my brother
2	was asleep in his bed.	sleeps in his bed.	were asleep in his bed.
3	At twelve o'clock	Tomorrow	Now
4	he's walking	he walked	he walks
5	across	downstairs	next to
6	and into the garden.	in the bedroom.	on the table.
7	He's climbing	He climbs	He climbed
8	the wall	the bathroom	the bed
9	and he finished	and he started	and he is
10	he sings.	sing.	to sing.
11	Now he is	Then he stopped	Then he walks
12	and in the garden.	and upstairs.	and walked back to bed.
13	In the morning	Yesterday afternoon	Tomorrow
14	you don't remember	he didn't remember	she didn't remember
15	my concert!	his concert!	your concert!

2 Choose the best title for the story.

The garden at night   A musical adventure   We love music

_____

10A Get moving!

1 Complete the crossword with means of transportation.

Across

2

3

4

Down

1

2

3

2 Work out Ana's trip. Number the pictures in order.

Big Smile Taxis

1:30 pm   April 14

JFK to Madison Hotel
First Avenue
$65.00

A

American Railroads

April 16
single
New York to Washington, D.C.

B

Ocean Airlines

Dulles Airport, Washington, D.C., to London Heathrow
Flight 349
April 17
depart: 9:35
arrive: 8:45 (local time)

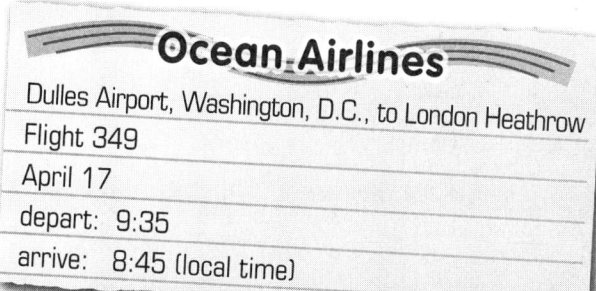

CITYBUS COMPANY

April 14
Central London
to Heathrow Airport
$6.95

D | 1

Manhattan Boat Tours

April 15 2:30 P.M.

1 trip around
Manhattan Island

E

Ocean Airlines

London Heathrow to JFK, New York
Flight 610
April 14
depart: 10:20
arrive: 11:30 (local time)

F

3 Write a sentence about each part of her trip.

1 First, she *took a bus to Heathrow Airport.*

2 Then *she* _____.

3 Then _____.

4 The next day _____.

5 On April 16 _____.

6 The next day _____.

10B A crazy vacation!

Part 1

1 Write a word for each description.

1   A month   _____
2   A number   _____
3   A type of transportation   _____
4   A weather adjective   _____
5   A vacation activity   _____
6   A food word   a _____
7   A food word   some _____
8   An adjective of feeling   _____
9   A weather adjective   _____
10 A store   _____

11 A color   _____
12 A clothes word   _____
13 A family word   _____
14 A vacation activity   go _____
15 An adjective of opinion   _____

✂ -

Part 2

2 Add your words to the story and read about your crazy vacation!

In ¹_____ I went on a vacation to Peru for ²_____ days. I took a ³_____ to Peru.

On the first day the weather was ⁴_____. I went ⁵_____. In the evening I went to a restaurant. I had ⁶_____ and ⁷_____. The meal was delicious! At the end of the day I was very ⁸_____.

On the second day it was ⁹_____. In the afternoon I went shopping. I went to a ¹⁰_____, and I bought a ¹¹_____ ¹²_____ for my ¹³_____. In the evening I decided to ¹⁴_____ with my new friends.

I went home on Saturday. My family liked their presents. I had a / an ¹⁵_____ vacation!

An active vacation

Student A

1 Look at the map and complete Jo's vacation activities for Monday, Wednesday, and Thursday.

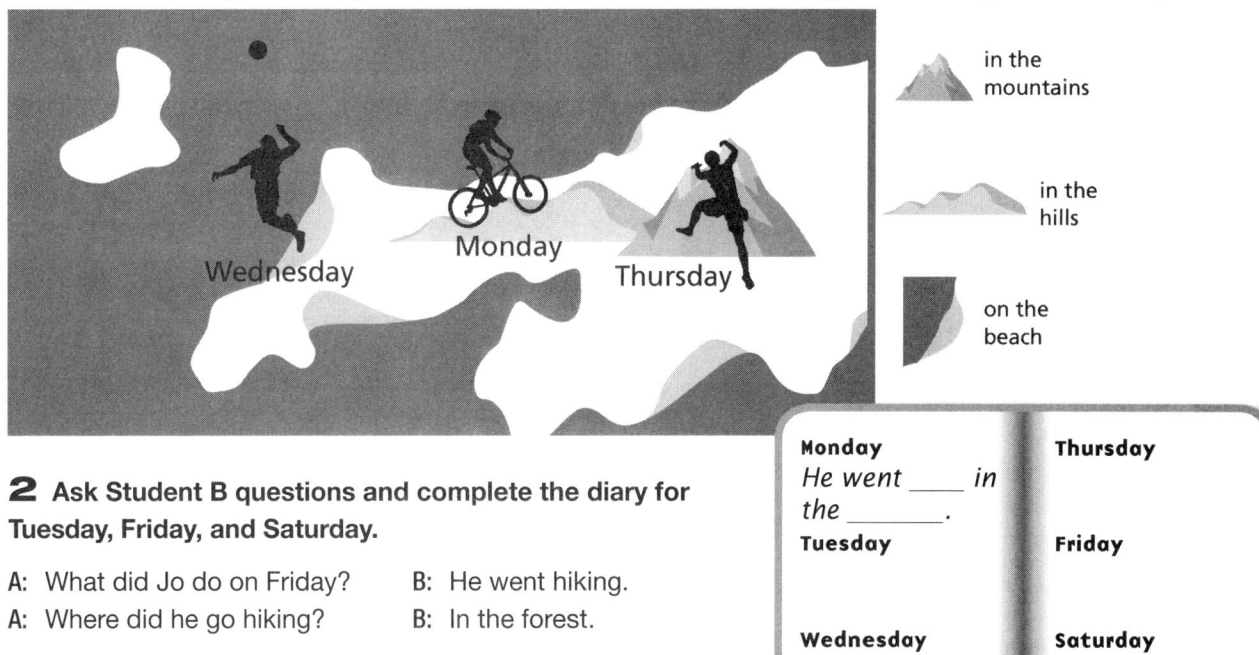

in the mountains

in the hills

on the beach

2 Ask Student B questions and complete the diary for Tuesday, Friday, and Saturday.

A: What did Jo do on Friday?   B: He went hiking.
A: Where did he go hiking?   B: In the forest.

3 Answer Student B's questions.

Monday	Thursday
He went ____ in the ____.	
Tuesday	**Friday**
Wednesday	**Saturday**

✂ -

Student B

1 Look at the map and complete Jo's vacation activities for Tuesday, Friday, and Saturday.

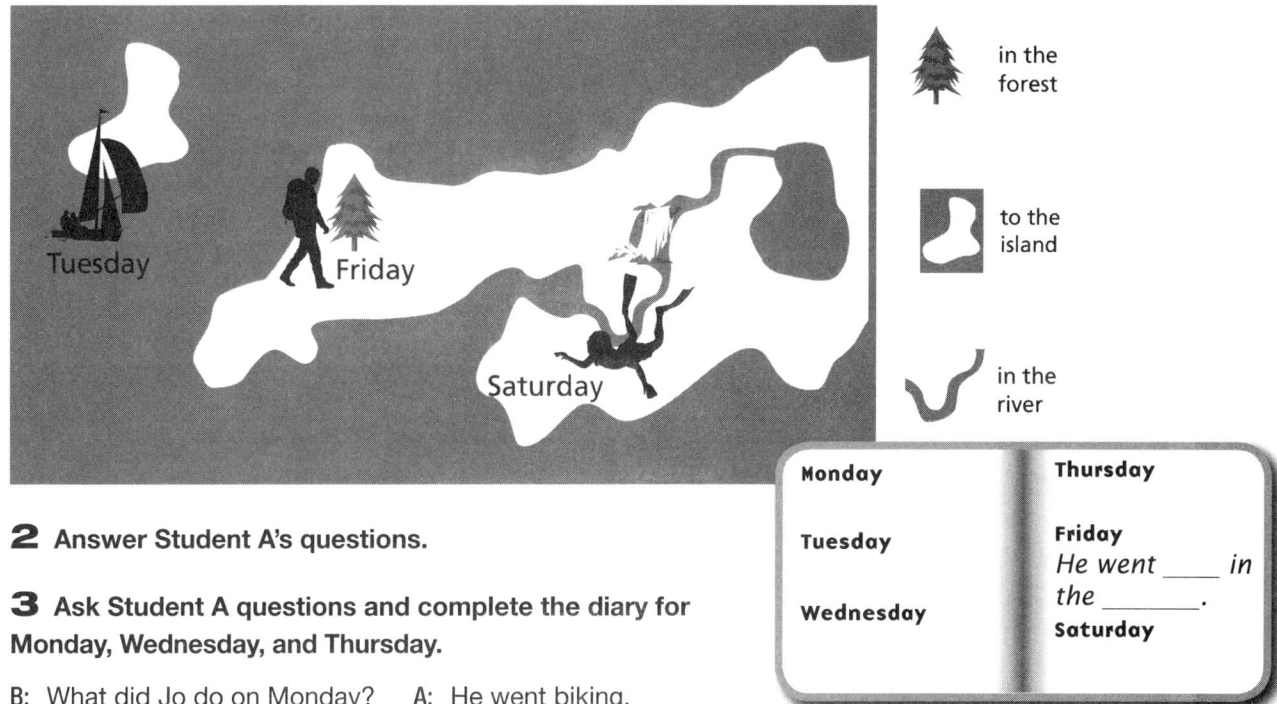

in the forest

to the island

in the river

2 Answer Student A's questions.

3 Ask Student A questions and complete the diary for Monday, Wednesday, and Thursday.

B: What did Jo do on Monday?   A: He went biking.
B: Where did he go biking?   A: In the hills.

Monday	Thursday
Tuesday	**Friday**
	He went ____ in the ____.
Wednesday	**Saturday**

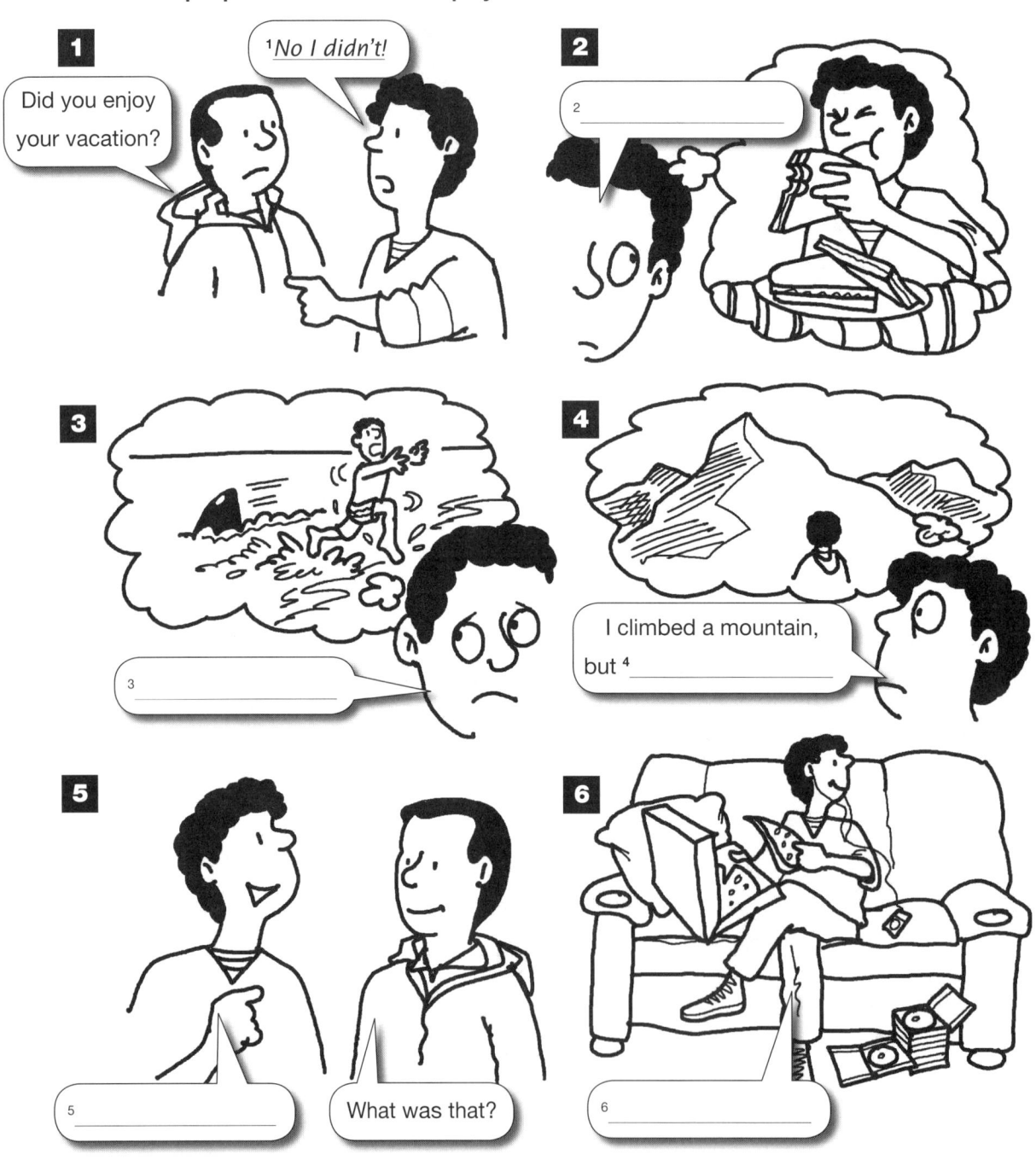

A bad vacation

Use the clues in the box to write complete sentences in the speech bubbles.
Use the simple past tense. Then role-play the conversation.

1

Did you enjoy your vacation?

¹*No I didn't!*

2

2 _____

3

3 _____

4

I climbed a mountain, but ⁴ _____

5

5 _____

What was that?

6

6 _____

a) I / not get / to the top

b) I / love / come / home

c) I / not like / the food

✓d) No / I / not

e) But / I / love / one thing

f) I / not swim / in the ocean

A celebrity wedding

1 Complete the story of Tom and Katie's wedding. Use the simple past of irregular verbs in the boxes.

A | found   took   ~~met~~   gave   rode

A few years ago, a famous Hollywood actor **¹** *met* a beautiful Hollywood actress. He was Tom Cruise. She was Katie Holmes. It was love at first sight.

On their first date, they **²**_____ a helicopter to the beach. Then they **³**_____ a motorcycle on the beach. Tom **⁴**_____ Katie a ring and asked her to marry him.

A few months later, they **⁵**_____ the perfect place for their wedding. It was the Odelaschio castle in Italy. They started to plan their wedding.

B | made   got   came

Tom and Katie **⁶**_____ married in November. A hundred and fifty guests **⁷**_____ to the wedding. The Italian designer Giorgio Armani **⁸**_____ Katie's wedding dress and Tom's suit.

C | sang   drove   left   had   cut

There was a party after the wedding. Tom and Katie **⁹**_____ a huge wedding cake, and Andrea Bocelli **¹⁰**_____ to the guests. They all **¹¹**_____ a great time.

Then Tom and Katie **¹²**_____ to Rome in their car. The guests **¹³**_____, too. It was a fantastic wedding!

2 Find the simple past forms of these verbs in the text. Read the mystery word and write it in the sentence. Then discover the mystery fact!

1 find

2 get

3 cut

4 ride

5 go

6 have

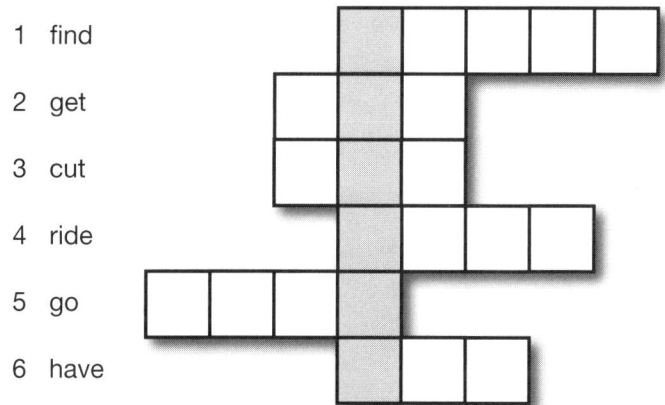

Circle every _____ word.

Katie   wedding   12   (October)   famous   film   November   10   Brazil

month   are   is   Germany   Kidman   Australia   Tom   Holmes   castle   Italy

Cruise   jump   Oprah   child   Day   Canada   third   15   in   newspaper

celebrity   angry   Japan   went   Nicole   daughter

11A Which is the best laptop?

1 Read about the laptop computers. Complete the paragraph with the names of the computers.

■■■■■■■■■■■
Which is the best laptop?
■■■■■■■■■■■

	Orion 225	Star Mini	QMT 894X	Alta 60N	Lightpro 1000
Screen Size	15 inch	12 inch	15 inch	17 inch	15 inch
Speed	**	**	*	*****	****
Weight	2.6 lb.	1.7 lb.	3.5 lb.	2.7 lb.	1.95 lb.
Extras	3 free computing lessons	10 free games	100 free tunes	none	100 free tunes, 10 free games; 1 free lesson
Price	$	$$	$$$	$$$$$	$$
Score	8.5	8.0	7.5	9.9	9.0

It's a difficult decision. The ¹ _Star Mini_ is the lightest and the smallest. The ² _____ has the best extras. The ³ _____ is the fastest, and it has the biggest screen. It's the best computer, but it isn't cheap. The cheapest computer is the ⁴ _____. It's faster than the QMT 894X and has a bigger screen than the ⁵ _____. It's a good buy if you don't have much money. We didn't like the ⁶ _____ because it's the slowest and the heaviest!

2 Match the people with the best computer for them.

1. I want the best computer. The price isn't a problem.

2. I want a computer for my music, and I want a fast computer.

3. I'm a beginner. I want to learn about computers.

4. I travel a lot, so I want a small, light computer.

5. I need a fast computer for games. I want a big screen, but I can't buy a very expensive computer.

1 _____ 2 _____ 3 _____ 4 _____ 5 _____

11B What's the best sport for you?

Student A

Read about the sports. Ask Student B questions and complete the chart.

A: Is skateboarding more difficult than windsurfing?   B: No, it isn't.

A: Is skiing the most difficult sport?   B: Yes, it is.

Choose your sport!

We asked a group of sports experts to give their opinion about three exciting sports. See what they decided about each one!

	Skateboarding	Windsurfing	Skiing
Difficult	★	★ ★	★ ★ ★
Dangerous	★ ★	★	★ ★ ★
Exciting			★ ★ ★
Expensive	★	★ ★	★ ★ ★
Fast	★		
Popular	★ ★ ★	★	★ ★

What's the best sport for you?

Student B

Read about the sports. Ask Student A questions and complete the chart.

B: Is skateboarding more dangerous than skiing?   A: No, it isn't.

B: Is skiing the most dangerous sport?   A: Yes, it is.

Choose your sport!

We asked a group of sports experts to give their opinion about three exciting sports. See what they decided about each one!

	Skateboarding	Windsurfing	Skiing
Difficult	★	★ ★	★ ★ ★
Dangerous	★ ★	★	★ ★ ★
Exciting	★	★ ★	★ ★ ★
Expensive			★ ★ ★
Fast	★	★ ★	★ ★ ★
Popular	★ ★ ★		

What's the best sport for you?

11c Clothesline

1 Write the clothes words in the word chains.

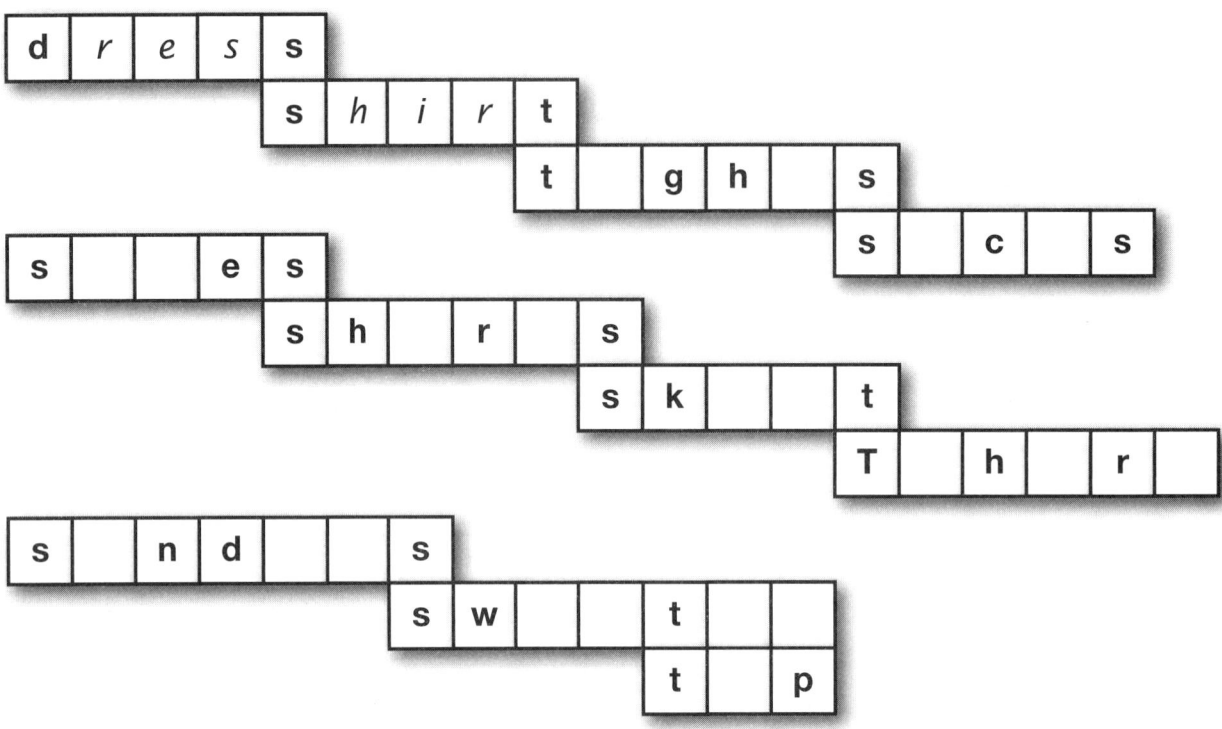

2 Make two clothes words from the letters in each circle.

1 b*oots*
2 b*elt*

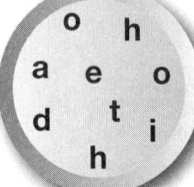

3 h_____
4 h_____

5 j_____
6 j_____

7 s_____
8 t_____

Shopping for shoes

Choose the correct phrase from the box. Write it in the speech bubble. Then role–play the conversation.

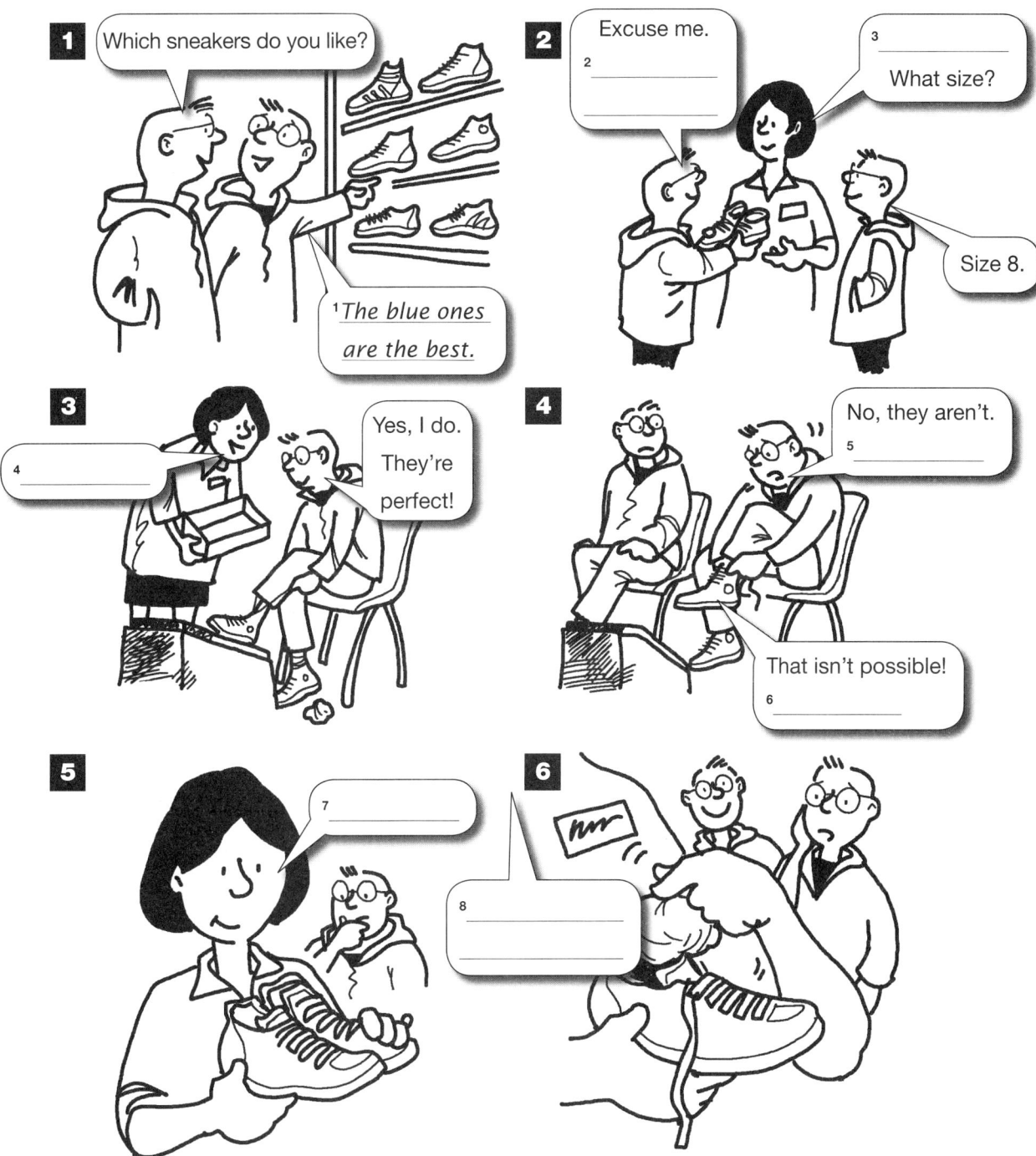

1 Which sneakers do you like?

¹The blue ones are the best.

2 Excuse me.

2 _____

3 _____ What size?

Size 8.

3 4 _____

Yes, I do. They're perfect!

4 No, they aren't.

5 _____

That isn't possible!

6 _____

5 7 _____

6 8 _____

a) Yes, of course.

b) Do you like them?

✓c) The blue ones are the best.

d) Can we try these on?

e) Wait a minute!

f) They're too small.

g) You didn't take the paper out!

h) We're identical twins!

The short adjective crossword

Complete the crossword with the opposite adjective, its comparative form, and its superlative form.

	Adjective	Comparative	Superlative
opposite of *hard*	14 across	9 down	6 across
opposite of *bad*	12 across	10 across	4 down
opposite of *small*	11 across	10 down	8 across
opposite of *cold*	7 across	3 across	1 down
opposite of *clean*	13 across	5 down	2 down

who's going to play?

Student A

Read about the musicians and singers. Ask Student B questions about them.
Add the information to the poster.

A: What kind of music does Kimeva sing?   B: She's an R&B singer.
A: How much are the tickets?   B: They're $25.
A: When are The Slide going to be at the Nitrogen Center?   B: On April 30.

Coming soon at the Nitrogen Center . . .

Kimeva
Poland's top ____R&B____ singer
Date: June 12
Tickets: _____

The Slide
A new heavy metal band from the U.S.
Date: _____
Tickets: $35

Chit Chat
Five-girl pop band from Australia
Date: _____
Tickets: $45

San Diego Sound
The world-famous _____ orchestra
Date: November 19
Tickets: _____

Student B

Read about the musicians and singers. Ask Student A questions about them.
Add the information to the poster.

B: When is Kimeva going to be at the Nitrogen Center?   A: On June 12.
B: What type of music do The Slide play?   A: They play heavy metal music.
B: How much are tickets for The Slide?   A: They're $35.

Coming soon at the Nitrogen Center . . .

Kimeva
Poland's top R&B singer
Date: *June 12*
Tickets: $25

The Slide
A new _____ band from the U.S.
Date: April 30
Tickets: _____

Chit Chat
Five-girl _____ band from Australia
Date: January 2
Tickets: _____

San Diego Sound
The world-famous Salsa orchestra
Date: _____
Tickets: $55

12B The story machine

Choose one box from each set and make a story. Write the story in the box.

1	Skier started	The skier started	The skier is starting
2	slow.	now.	slowly.
3	Then he did	Then he went	Then he goes
4	very fast	up	past
5	and he jumps	and he is jumping	and he jumped
6	very well.	good.	again.
7	He didn't	He landed	He lands
8	bad.	well.	good.
9	The crowd shouted	The crowd was	The crowd listened
10	noisy.	loudly.	slowly.
11	His	Her	Its
12	to jump	jumped	jump
13	were	was	is
14	a new	a newer	an old
15	one!	world record!	ones!

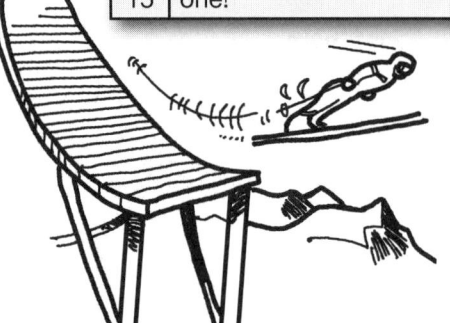

An Amazing Jump!

The skier started slowly.

12c The talent show

Make sentences using the word clues in the box. Write the sentences in the speech bubbles. Then role-play the conversation.

1

FIND A STAR

¹*I want to win this competition!*

2

And the next contestant is . . . Luke!

2 _____

_____, Luke?

3 _____

3

Oh . . . Love hurts a lot . . .

Be careful! 4 _____

_____!

4

Ow! It hurts . . . Ouch!

5

Ow! Love . . . Ow! Ouch!

He's awesome!

It's amazing!

5 _____

6

a) What / you / going / sing

✓b) I / want / win / this competition

c) You / going / hit / the wasp

d) I / going / sing / "Love hurts a lot."

e) I / want / cry

Motivator quiz: Music

Answer the questions. Check your answers and write your score.

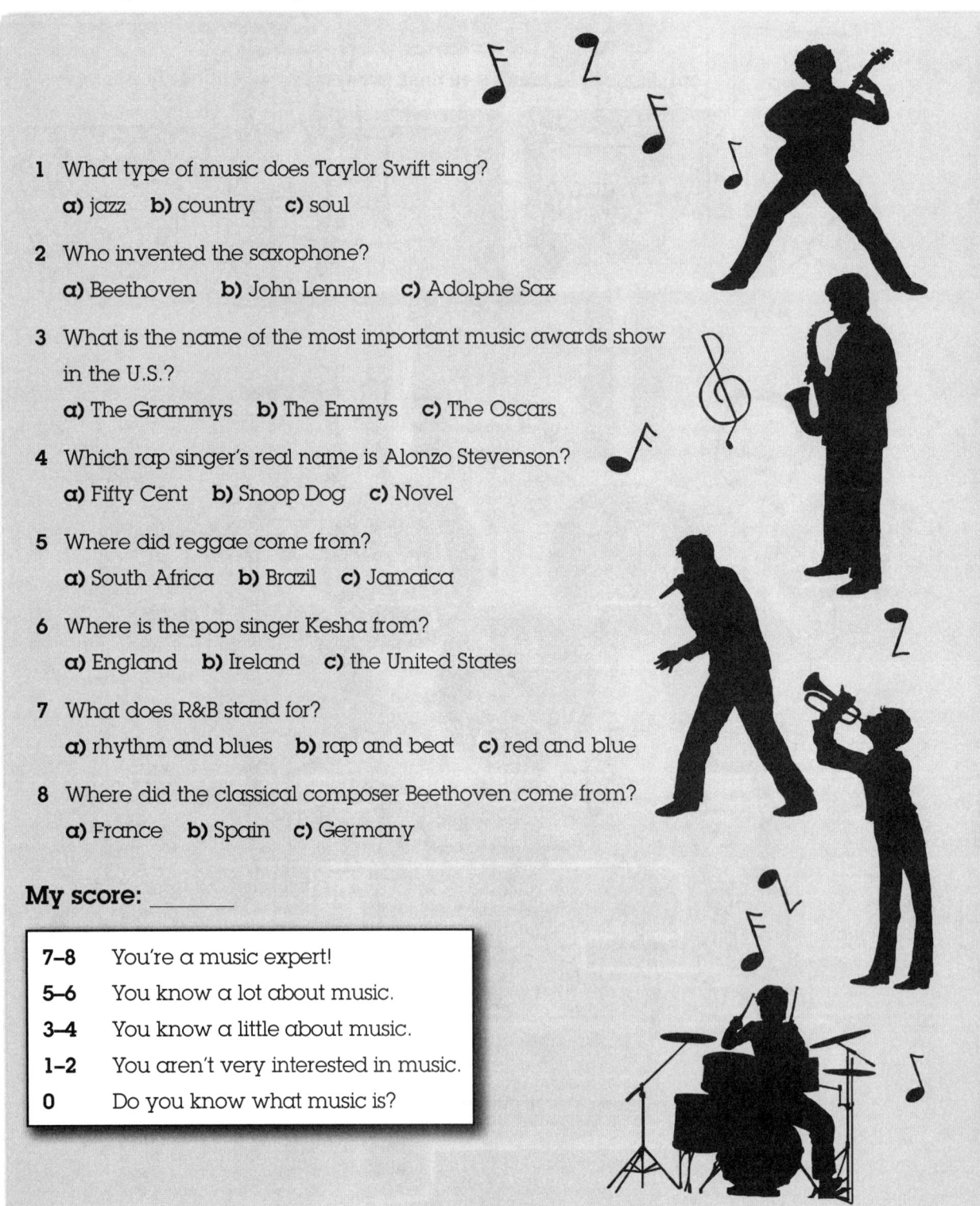

1 What type of music does Taylor Swift sing?

   a) jazz   **b)** country   **c)** soul

2 Who invented the saxophone?

   a) Beethoven   **b)** John Lennon   **c)** Adolphe Sax

3 What is the name of the most important music awards show in the U.S.?

   a) The Grammys   **b)** The Emmys   **c)** The Oscars

4 Which rap singer's real name is Alonzo Stevenson?

   a) Fifty Cent   **b)** Snoop Dog   **c)** Novel

5 Where did reggae come from?

   a) South Africa   **b)** Brazil   **c)** Jamaica

6 Where is the pop singer Kesha from?

   a) England   **b)** Ireland   **c)** the United States

7 What does R&B stand for?

   a) rhythm and blues   **b)** rap and beat   **c)** red and blue

8 Where did the classical composer Beethoven come from?

   a) France   **b)** Spain   **c)** Germany

My score: _____

7–8	You're a music expert!
5–6	You know a lot about music.
3–4	You know a little about music.
1–2	You aren't very interested in music.
0	Do you know what music is?

Famous people . . . who aren't famous!

**Complete the profiles with the words in the boxes. Then solve the code
to find an unusual fact about each person.**

A Shigeru Miyamoto

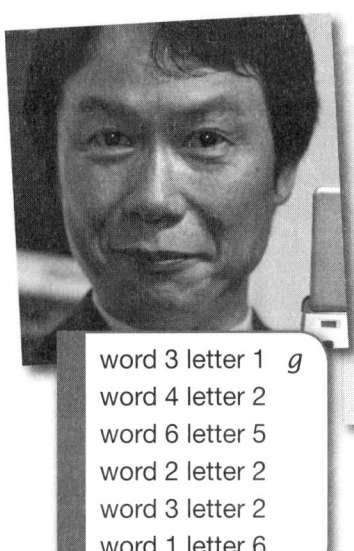

| games   success   working   ~~father~~   were   started |

Shigeru Miyamoto is from Japan. People call him "the ¹*father* of video games."
In 1977 he ² _____ working for a small Japanese company called
Nintendo. The company made card games, and it wasn't very successful.
They started to make video ³ _____, and in 1980 Shigeru created *Donkey
Kong*. It was a ⁴ _____ all over the world. After that, Shigeru created the
famous Mario games. These ⁵ _____ the most popular video games in
the world for many years. He's still ⁶ _____ on games today.

word 3 letter 1	*g*
word 4 letter 2	
word 6 letter 5	
word 2 letter 2	
word 3 letter 2	
word 1 letter 6	

In his free time Shigeru doesn't play video games.
He plays the _____.

B Matt Groening

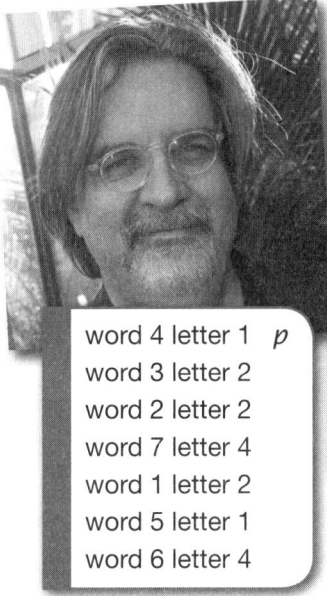

| people   was   draw   more   ~~in~~   television   first |

Matt Groening is the man behind *The Simpsons*. He created Homer, Marge,
Bart, Lisa, and Maggie ¹*in* 1985. It took him ten minutes to ² _____ them!
The first episodes were on Fox TV in 1987. It ³ _____ an instant success.

Every week more than 60 million ⁴ _____ around the world watch *The
Simpsons*. It's the most popular show in the history of ⁵ _____. In 2007
Matt Groenig produced the ⁶ _____ Simpsons movie. There are going
to be ⁷ _____ Simpsons movies in the future.

word 4 letter 1	*p*
word 3 letter 2	
word 2 letter 2	
word 7 letter 4	
word 1 letter 2	
word 5 letter 1	
word 6 letter 4	

Homer and Marge are the names of Matt's _____.

Teacher's notes and Answer keys

1A Celebrity soccer team

Aims: To practice the verb *to be* (singular), possessive adjectives (singular), and question formation

Instructions: • Give each student a photocopy of the worksheet. • Draw students' attention to the example in item 1 (Cameron Diaz) and go through it with them. • Explain that students first must unscramble the celebrity names. • They then look at the information about birthdays to figure out how old the celebrities are. • Using this information and the words in the box at the top of the page, students complete the conversations.

> **Answer key:** 1 she 2 Cameron Diaz 3 old
> 4 (current age) 5 What's 6 Beyoncé 7 How
> 8 (current age) 9 Who's 10 Enrique Iglesias 11 he
> 12 (current age) 13 her 14 Hilary Duff 15 She's
> 16 (current age) 17 Kylie Minogue 18 is 19 She's
> 20 (current age) 21 your 22 Michael Phelps 23 are
> 24 (current age) 25 name 26 My 27 Angelina Jolie
> **Ex 2** Beckham 28 (current age) 29 I'm

1B People puzzle!

Aims: To understand personal information – names, addresses, telephone numbers, and ages

Instructions: • Show students the information in the table. • Read the information about Mrs. K. Jones (her address and phone number) and show students how to add this information to the table. • Students read the rest of the information and complete the table.

> **Answer key:** 1 Jackie / Meakin / 33614 / 813-555-
> 0144 / 16 / Monday; 2 Peter / Roberts / 33601 /
> 813-555-2287 / 25 / Tuesday and Friday; 3 Karen /
> Jones / 33601 / 813-555-0102 / 31 / Wednesday and
> Saturday; 4 John / Meakin / 33601 / 813-464-0132 /
> 17 / Thursday and Sunday

1C Musicians around the world

Aims: To practice the verb *to be* (plural), *Where ... from?* questions, and vocabulary for countries

Instructions: Ex 1 • Read the first conversation (about the Toon Boys) to students. • Show

students the line from the picture of the musicians to Newcastle, the town in England. • Students read the other five conversations and draw lines from the pictures to the correct towns.

Ex 2 • Show students the letters next to the towns. • Students write the letters in the boxes. • Students rearrange the letters to make the name of a country. They add the name to the poster.

> **Answer key: Ex 1** The Toon Boys – R,
> Mobile Tones – B, Fernando Santos – A, Natalia
> Alessi - L, Marek Kopolski – Z, Green Dream – I
> **Ex 2** Brazil

1D Consolidation 1 Words, words, words!

Aims: To review the vocabulary for countries, nationalities, numbers, and days of the week

Instructions: Ex 1 • Read the headings in the chart (*First letter, Country, Nationality,* etc.) to students. • Show students that in the first row, all the words begin with letter *t*. • Ask students to suggest words for items 1 and 2 in the first row (*thirty, Thursday*). • Students complete the rest of the words in the table.

Ex 2 • Read the clue for 1 across (*a country*) to students. • Show students 1 across in the crossword, and point out the first letter (*R*) and the number of letters needed (6). • Students write in the answer (*Russia*). • Students complete the rest of the crossword.

> **Answer key: Ex 1** 1 thirty 2 Thursday 3 French
> 4 five 5 forty 6 Spanish 7 six 8 seven 9 sixteen
> 10 seventeen 11 sixty 12 seventy
> 13 Saturday Sunday
> **Ex 2** Across: 1 Russia 2 eighteen 3 eleven 4 Japan
> 5 ninety; Down: 3 eight 6 Friday 7 Brazil 8 nineteen
> 9 Portugal 10 Wednesday

1D Consolidation 2 Who are they?

Aims: To review asking for and giving personal information, and saying numbers, letters, phone numbers, zip codes, and addresses

Instructions: • Make a photocopy of the worksheet for each pair of students. • Cut the worksheets in half along the dotted line. • Arrange students in pairs. One student in each pair is Student A, the other is Student B. • Give each student a Student A section or a Student B section. • Show students that there is information about Boy X and Girl Y on the worksheets. • Read the first example question for Student A (*What's his name?*) and ask a Student B to answer it (*Pedro*). Show students where to write the information on the worksheet. • Read the first example question for Student B (*How old is he?*) and ask a Student A to answer it (*17*). Show students where to write the information on the worksheet. • Students take turns asking and answering the questions in pairs and writing the information on their worksheets.

> **Answer key:** This is Pedro. He's 17. He's from Chile. His address in the U.S. is 40 Longwood Street, Chicago, IL. His zip code is 60605. His phone number is 312-555-7720. This is Sandra. She's 14. She's from Poland. Her address in the U.S. is 96 Greendale Street, Chicago, IL. Her zip code is 60605. Her phone number is 312-268-8115.

2A Mystery objects

Aims: To practice vocabulary for common objects and *this, that, these, those*

Instructions: Ex 1 • Point to the picture in number 1 and ask, *What are these? (apples).* • Show students that the letters for *apples* have been crossed out in the scrambled letters. • Show students the word *apples* under *Picture word*. • Ask, *What extra letters are there?* (B, G, A). • Show students the extra word (*bag*) that is made from these scrambled letters. • Students figure out the other picture words and extra words.

Ex 2 • Point to the first picture. Read the example question and answer. • Point to the second picture. Ask students to say the question (*What's this?*) and answer (*It's a T-shirt.*). • Students write the questions and answers.

> **Answer key: Ex 1** 1 apples, bag 2 camera, watch 3 sneakers, hats 4 keys, pens 5 T-shirt, books
> **Ex 2** 1 What are these? They're apples. 2 What's this? It's a T-shirt. 3 What's this? It's a camera. 4 What are these? They're sneakers. 5 What are these? They're keys.

2B What color is that?

Aims: To practice vocabulary for personal possessions and colors, and the possessive *'s*

Instructions: • Read the names (*Darren, Natalie,* etc.) to students. • Follow the line from Darren to the relevant object and ask, *What is it? (a phone).* • Point out the scrambled letters and ask, *What color is it? (black).* • Show students the color word *black* on the answer line next to the scrambled words. • Show students the example sentence (*Darren's phone is black.*). • Students follow the other lines, write the colors, and write the sentences.

> **Answer key:** 1 Darren's phone is black. 2 Natalie's sneakers are brown. 3 Her friend's T-shirt is pink. 4 His brothers' hats are gray. 5 His sisters' backpack are purple.

2C How much is it?

Aims: To practice vocabulary for fast food and drinks and to ask about prices

Instructions: • Make a photocopy of the worksheet for each pair of students. • Cut the worksheets in half along the dotted line. • Arrange students in pairs. One student in each pair is Student A, the other is Student B. • Give each student a Student A section or a Student B section.

Ex 1 • Show students there is information about the food and the prices in both sections. • Read the example question for Student A (*How much is a cheese sandwich?*) and ask a Student B to answer it. (*It's $4.50.*) • Show students how to write the information in the menu. • Read the example question for Student B (*How much is a chicken sandwich?*) and ask a Student A to answer it. (*It's $5.50.*) • Show students how to write the information in the menu. • Students take turns to ask and answer the questions in pairs. They write the information in their menus.

Ex 2 • Write the first incomplete bill for Student A on the board. • Help students to figure out the missing item. They should figure out the price of the missing item first (*$3.75*) and then see what item is that price

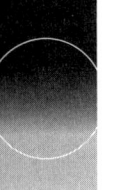

(*burger*). • Students figure out the other items in the other bills.

> **Answer key: Ex 1** Food/Snacks: Chicken sandwich $5.50, Cheese sandwich $4.50, Burger $3.75, Hot dog $1.75, Potato chips 75¢, Ice cream $2.00
> Drinks: Soda 75¢, Bottled water $1.00, Orange juice $1.50, Hot chocolate $1.50, Tea $1.00, Coffee $1.50
> **Ex 2** Student A: 1 Burger / $3.75, 2 Cheese sandwich / $4.50, 3 Potato chips / 75¢
> Student B: 1 Soda / 75¢, 2 Hot dog / $1.75, 3 Ice cream / $2.00

2D Consolidation 1 At the deli

Aims: To review ordering food in a deli, and to role-play a conversation

Instructions: • Read the sentences in the box to students. • Show students the example answer in 1 (*Can I have a cheese sandwich . . .?*). • Ask students to find the correct sentence for 2, using the picture to help them. • Students complete the rest of the story. • Choose three students and assign a character (boy, friend, assistant) to each. • The three students read and role-play the conversation.

> **Answer key:** 1 b) Can I have a cheese sandwich and a chicken sandwich, please? 2 a) Here you go. 3 f) This is your sandwich. This is my sandwich. 4 e) How much is that? 5 h) $9.25 6 c) Thank you. 7 g) Where's my sandwich? 8 d) Oh, sorry.

2D Consolidation 2 Motivator quiz: General knowledge

Aims: To review the language of the unit

Instructions: • Explain the idea of *general knowledge* to students; ask them to say, in their own words, the type of questions you find in a general knowledge quiz (*What is the capital of …? / How high is …? / Who is …?*). • Read the first question to students and ask them to suggest the answer. • Students answer the rest of the questions individually. • Go through the correct answers with students (see Answer key). • Students figure out their score. • Congratulate students with a score of 7–8.

> **Answer key:** 1 b) 2 c) 3 a) 4 c) 5 b) 6 c) 7 b) 8 a)

3A In a house

Aims: To practice vocabulary for rooms, parts of a house, furnishings, and fixtures

Instructions: Ex 1 • Point to number 1 in the picture and ask, *What is it?* (*the kitchen*) • Show students that number 1 in the crossword is completed with *kitchen*. • Point to number 2 in the picture and ask, *What is it?* (*dishwasher*). • Help students to find number 2 in the crossword; students write *dishwasher* in the crossword. • Students complete the rest of the crossword.

Ex 2 • Show students that some squares in the crossword are gray. • Students write the letters that are in these squares into the boxes in Ex 2. • Students unscramble the letters to form a word.

> **Answer Key: Ex 1** 1 kitchen 2 dishwasher
> 3 bathroom 4 shower 5 toilet 6 stove 7 bedroom
> 8 window 9 door 10 sink 11 lamp 12 refrigerator
> **Ex 2** washing machine

3B Find the furniture

Aims: To practice furniture vocabulary

Instructions: Ex 1 • Ask an individual student to find the first word in the word ribbon (*desk*). • Show students the example circle around *desk*. • Students then circle all the other words in the word ribbon.

Ex 2 • Explain that some of the letters in the word ribbon have symbols. • Show students the first letter with a symbol tag (*e*, with the ● tag). • Show students how to write *e* in a box under the ● symbol. • Repeat with the next letter in the word ribbon with a symbol tag (*o*, with the ✳ tag). • Show students how to write *o* in a box under the ✳ symbol. • Students add the rest of the letters with symbols to the boxes. • Show students that the letters have been rearranged to make the first word (*What's*). • Students make words from the other scrambled letters and read the question (*What's your favorite possession?*). • Students write their answer to the question. • Students ask each other the question and answer it.

3C Where are they?

Aims: To practice prepositions of place

Instructions: • Make a photocopy of the worksheet for each pair of students. • Cut the worksheets in half along the dotted line. • Arrange students in pairs. One student in each pair is Student A, the other is Student B. • Give each student a Student A section or a Student B section.

Ex 1 • Show students that they both have the same pictures of students at Hill Road High School. They need to find out and write the names of the students. • Read the example question for Student A (*Where's Sanjay?*) and ask a Student B to answer it. Show students how to figure out where Sanjay is. • Read the example question for Student B (*Where's Charlene?*) and ask a Student A to answer it. Show students how to figure out where Charlene is. • Students take turns to ask and answer the questions in pairs. They write the names. (Note that there are different ways of describing each position; sometimes students will have to try different descriptions in order to help their partner.)

Ex 2 • Students identify the two objects in their section, then ask questions to find where the objects are in their partner's picture.

3D Consolidation 1 What's your style?

Aims: To review *There is … / There are …, some* and *any*, and vocabulary for furniture and objects

Instructions: • Show students the two living rooms. • Read the two example sentences. • Say, *Can*

you find other differences? Students suggest other differences, for example, *There is a table in A. There isn't a table in B.* • Show students how to write the two sentences under A and B. • Student find seven more differences.

3D Consolidation 2 Call your phone!

Aims: To review making and responding to requests, and to role-play a conversation

Instructions: • Read the sentences in the box to students. • Show students the example answer in 1 (*Where's my cell phone?*). • Ask students to find the correct sentence for 2. • Students complete the rest of the story. • Choose three students and assign a character (girl, boy 1, and boy 2) to each. • The three students read and role-play the conversation.

4A Jack's big blog

Aims: To practice vocabulary for family members

Instructions: Ex 1 • Point to the family tree and ask questions about it, such as, *Who are Jack's uncles?* (*Neil and Alfonso*) and *What is the name of Jack's grandmother?* (*Susana*). • Ask a student to start reading the text from Jack's blog. The student adds the missing word to the second sentence (*sister*). • Students complete the rest of the paragraph.

Ex 2 • Read the first clue for the grid (*Craig is Jack's …*). • Students complete the sentence (*brother*) and write the word in the grid. • Students complete the rest of the grid. • Students read the mystery word and write it on the answer line.

> **Answer key: Ex 1** 1 Craig 2 sister 3 uncle 4 aunt
> 5 wife 6 daughters / children 7 cousins 8 husband
> 9 only child 10 grandparents
> **Ex 2** 1 brother 2 uncle 3 mother 4 grandfather
> 5 daughter 6 nephew 7 parents
> He is a blogger.

4B What do they have?

Aims: To practice appearance vocabulary and *have* with descriptions of people

Instructions: Ex 1 • Read the first sentence in the description. • Show students the chart. Point to the ✗ in the box for *long hair* and the ✓ in the box for *beard*. • Students add the rest of the information in the text to the table, so that every box has a ✓ or a ✗.

Ex 2 • Point to picture A and ask questions such as *Does he have curly hair?* and *Does he have a beard?* • Students figure out who it is (*Andrew*) and write the name on the answer line. • Students figure out the rest of the names.

Ex 3 • Ask individual students each to read a sentence from the speech bubble. • Students figure out who Tito's cousin is. • They complete the sentence with the person's name.

> **Answer key: Ex 1** Tito ✗ ✓ ✗ ✓ Oscar ✗ ✓ ✓ ✗
> Andrew ✗ ✗ ✓ ✗ Linda ✓ ✗ ✓ Liz ✗ ✗ ✓ Jill ✓ ✓ ✗
> **Ex 2** A Andrew B Liz C Jill D Tito E Linda F Oscar
> **Ex 3** Linda

4C Celebrity birthdays

Aims: To practice vocabulary for months and ordinal numbers vocabulary

Instructions: • Make a photocopy of the worksheet for each pair of students. • Cut the worksheets in half along the dotted line. • Arrange students in pairs. One student in each pair is Student A, the other is Student B. • Give each student a Student A section or a Student B section.

Ex 1 • Explain to students that each section has the same celebrity names, but different information about their birthdays. • Ask a Student A and a Student B to read the example questions and answers for Student A (*When is George Clooney's birthday?* etc.). • Show students the example answers in the table. • Ask a Student B and a Student A to read the example questions and answers for Student B (*When is Justin Timberlake's birthday?* etc.). • Show students the example answers in the table. • Students take turns to ask and answer the questions in pairs. They write the information in their tables.

Ex 2 • Show students how to write a list of the birthdays in date order through the year, starting with the example. • Students write the celebrity names and add each celebrity's letter. • Students read the name of the mystery celebrity.

> **Answer key: Ex 1** George Clooney I May 6 / Justin Timberlake A January 31 / Mariah Carey R March 27 / Brad Pitt D December 18 / Avril Lavigne O September 27 / Johnny Depp S June 9 / Lindsay Lohan O July 2 / Daniel Radcliffe N July 23 / Orlando Bloom H January 13 / Cameron Diaz F August 30 / Scarlett Johansson R November 22 / Bruce Willis R March 19
> **Ex 2** Orlando Bloom H January 13 / Justin Timberlake A January 31 / Bruce Willis R March 19 /Mariah Carey R March 27 / George Clooney I May 6 / Johnny Depp S June 9 / Lindsay Lohan O July 2 / Daniel Radcliffe N July 23 / Cameron Diaz F August 30 / Avril Lavigne O September 27 / Scarlett Johansson R November 22 / Brad Pitt D December 18 /
>
> The mystery celebrity is Harrison Ford.

4D Consolidation 1 The mystery birthday cake

Aims: To review conversational phrases and family vocabulary, and to role-play a conversation

Instructions: • Read the sentences in the box to students. • Show students the example answer in 1 (*Is it your grandmother's birthday?*). • Ask students to find the correct sentence for 2, using the picture to help them. • Students complete the rest of the story. • Choose two students and assign a character (boy, girl) to each. • The two students read and role-play the conversation.

4D Consolidation 2 Motivator quiz: Popular culture

Aims: To review the language of the unit

Instructions: • Explain the idea of *popular culture*
to students; ask them to say, in their own words,
the type of questions you find in a popular culture
quiz (*What was the name of Lady Gaga's first hit?*
etc.). • Read the first question to students and ask
them to suggest the answer. • Students answer the
rest of the questions individually. • Go through the
correct answers with students (see Answer key).
• Students figure out their score. • Congratulate
students with a score of 7–8.

5A He's a plumber.

Aims: To practice vocabulary for jobs and
countries, and the simple present

Instructions: Ex 1 • Show students the word
secretary circled in the word search puzzle.
• Students circle nine more jobs in the word
search puzzle.

Ex 2 • Point to the scrambled letters in #1 and ask,
What is the occupation? (salesclerk) • Students then
look at the other scrambled words examples and
write the name of each occupation.

Ex 3 • Point to the first picture. Ask, *Who is he?*
(*Max*). • Read the sentence about him (*I fix kitchens
and bathrooms*). • Ask, *What is his job?* (*plumber*).
• Point to the country name under Max's photo
and ask, *Where does the plumber live?* (*France*). •
Read the example answer in 1 (*Max is a plumber.
He lives in France.*). • Students read the rest of the
sentences, figure out what each person does, where
he or she lives, and write a sentence about it.

5B What do they do?

Aims: To practice vocabulary for places of work
and jobs, and the simple present

Instructions: • Make a photocopy of the
worksheet for each pair of students. • Cut the
worksheets in half along the dotted line. • Arrange
students in pairs. One student in each pair is
Student A, the other is Student B. • Give each
student a Student A section or a Student B section.
• Explain to students that each section has the
same names, but different information about the
people's jobs, place of work, etc. • Ask a Student A
and a Student B to read the example question and
answer for Student A (*What does Mario do? He's
an artist.*). • Show students the example answer
in the table. • Ask a Student B and a Student A to
read the example question and answer for Student
B (*Where does Mario work? He works in a studio.*).
• Show students the example answer in the chart. •
The Ss take turns to ask and answer the questions
in pairs. They write the information in their charts.

5C I love it!

Aims: To practice object pronouns

Instructions: Ex 1 • Point to each of the pictures and
texts. Ask individual students to read them to the class.

Ex 2 • Point to the first picture at the bottom of the page. Ask, *Who is it?* (*Emma*). Ask, *Who is she thinking about?* (*Tom*). Ask, *What else is she thinking about?* (*The London Eye*). • Read the example sentence. • Point out the use of *him*. • Students write the other sentences, using pronouns.

> **Answer key: Ex 2** 1 She likes him. 2 She likes it.
> 3 She likes her. 4 She doesn't like him. 5 She likes it.
> 6 He likes them. 7 He doesn't like it.

5D Consolidation 1 Who is the mystery guest?

Aims: To review conversational phrases and to role-play a conversation

Instructions: • Read the sentences in the box to students. • Show students the example answer in 1 (*Is he an actor?*). • Ask students to find the correct sentence for 2. • Students complete the rest of the conversation. They guess the name of the celebrity and write it in 6. • Choose two students and assign a character (quiz show host, girl) to each. • The two students read and role-play the conversation.

> **Answer key:** 1 b) Is he an actor? 2 e) Yes, he is.
> 3 d) Yes, he does. He's from Spain. 4 c) Is his wife Spanish, too? 5 a) Does he like soccer? 6 Antonio Banderas

5D Consolidation 2 My job is great!

Aims: To review vocabulary for jobs and places of work, and adjectives of opinion

Instructions: Ex 1 • Point to the first picture and ask, *What's her job?* (*a waitress*). • Show students the letters for *waitress* crossed out in the first set of scrambled letters. • Ask, *Where does she work?* (*in a restaurant*). • Show students the letters for *restaurant* crossed out in the second set of scrambled letters. • Explain to students that there are some extra letters, which they will use in Ex 2. Show students these extra letters in the circle in row 1. • Students cross out the other letters for jobs and for places of work. • They write the words for the jobs and the places of work on the answer lines. • They write the extra letter in the circles.

Ex 2 • Point to row 1 in Ex 1 again. • Say, *Make an adjective with these letters.* (*terrible*) • Point to the picture of the waitress in Ex 2. Read the example sentence (*My job is terrible.*). • Students rearrange the other letters from Ex 1 to make adjectives, and write them.

> **Answer key: Ex 1** 1 waitress, restaurant 2 doctor, hospital 3 secretary, office 4 teacher, school
> 5 sales clerk, store
> **Ex 2** 1 terrible 2 amazing 3 boring 4 great 5 good

6A A day out

Aims: To practice vocabulary for time and the simple present with fixed times

Instructions: Ex 1 • Point to the schedules and advertisements on the page. Ask questions about each one, such as, *What time does the first film start at the Moviezone Cinema?* (*At 10:20 A.M.*), *What time does the last train leave from Oakland to San Francisco?* (*At 7:50 P.M.*) and *When can you get two hamburgers for the price of one at Mike Donald's?* (*From 1:30 P.M. to 2:30 P.M.*). • Read the information in the box at the top of the page to students. • Point to the missing lines in the train timetable. Ask, *What time does the first train leave from San Francisco?*
• Explain how to figure out the answer: the first train arrives at 8:20 A.M. The train ride is fifteen minutes. So it leaves San Francisco at 8:05 A.M. • Students add the missing times to the schedules and advertisements.

Ex 2 • Read the information in the box to students. Explain that Julio and Matt have to go from San Francisco to Oakland by train, do all the activities in Oakland, then return to San Francisco by train.
• In pairs, students figure out a timetable so that they can do all the things. (Note that the times students suggest may vary slightly.)

> **Answer key: Ex 1** 1 12:55 2 12:10 3 4:50 4 8:05
> 5 9:05 6 7:30 7 7:25 8 6:30 9 12:45
> **Ex 2** 1 Train to Oakland 8:25–8:40 2 Exhibition at the Oakland Museum 8:55–9:55 3 Movie at Moviezone 10:20–11:30 4 Lunch at Mike Donald's 11:45–12:30 5 Concert at Snow Park 12:45–2:45 6 Football game at the Oakland Coliseum 3:00–6:30 7 Train to San Francisco 7:10–7:25

6B One boy's day

Aims: To practice vocabulary for daily routines

Instructions: • Read what the boy says about his day. • Show students how to follow the line from the top of the page down to *eat breakfast*. Ask, *What time does he have breakfast?* • Explain that it must be 8:00, because he goes to school at 8:30. • Ask, *What's the letter?* (D). • Students then follow the rest of the lines, choose the correct times, and circle the letter. • Students read the boy's name and write it on the answer line.

> **Answer key:** 8:00 (D), 2:15 (A), 4:00 (V), 7:30 (I), 10:00 (D) The boy's name is David.

6C At the gym

Aims: To practice adverbial phrases of frequency

Instructions: • Read the first clue to students (*Rosa goes to the gym …* etc.). • Point to the pictures of the people at the gym and ask, *Which person is Rosa?* Students figure out which person is Rosa (she's at the gym on Monday, but she isn't in any of the other pictures, because she only goes once a week). • Students find Rosa in pictures 1–8 at the bottom of the page (she's number 4). They write her name on the answer line. • Students read the rest of the sentences and write the names under the pictures.

> **Answer key:** 1 Tito 2 Joe 3 Alice 4 Rosa 5 Rafa 6 Naomi 7 Carlos 8 Carol

6D Consolidation 1 A word game

Aims: To review vocabulary for daily routines

Instructions: • Make a photocopy of the worksheet for each pair of students. • Cut the worksheets in half along the dotted line. • Arrange students in pairs. One student in each pair is Student A, the other is Student B. • Give each student a Student A section or a Student B section.

Ex 1 • Show students that they have two charts on their worksheet. One chart is the words they are going to collect (*Your words*). The other chart is the words they are going to give to their partner.

• Borrow a card from a Student A. Say, *I am Student A*. Say *B3* to a Student B. The student replies with the word in B3 (*get*). • Show students the example answer *get* in the B3 box in the *Your words* chart. The Student As then ask the Student Bs for words to complete their chart.

Ex 2 • Borrow a card from a Student B. Say, *I am Student B*. Say, *C4* to a Student A. The student replies with the words in C4 (*in bed*). • Show students the example answer *in bed* in the C4 box in the *Your words* chart • The Student Bs then ask the Student As for words to complete their chart.

Ex 3 • Explain to students that they have a mix of verbs and nouns in their charts. • Show students how to combine the verbs and nouns to make daily routines, for example, *eat lunch, eat dinner,* etc. • Give students one minute to make as many combinations for daily routines as they can.

> **Answer key: Ex 3** go to school, go to bed, go to sleep, call a friend, eat breakfast, eat lunch, eat dinner, get up, get to school, get in bed, get to sleep, read in bed, play video games (Other combinations are possible.)

6D Consolidation 2 Are they identical?

Aims: To review the simple present with vocabulary for times and daily routines, and to role-play a conversation

Instructions: Ex 1 • Read the phrases for daily routines in the box to students. • Show students the example answer in 1 (*get up*). • Ask students to find the correct answer for 2. • Students complete the rest of the story. • Ask a student to read the question in the speech bubble at the top of the page. • Ask students to answer the question, using information from the story. • Choose three students and assign a character (interviewer, Tim, Tony) to each. • The three students read and role-play the conversation.

Ex 2 • Read the sentences in 1 to students, including the example answer (*Tony gets up*

at seven thirty.). • Remind students about their answer to the question about Tim and Tony in Ex 1. • Students complete the rest of the sentences with the information about Tony.

Answer key: Ex 1 1 c) get up 2 d) gets up 3 e) brush my teeth 4 f) brushes his teeth 5 b) eat breakfast 6 a) eat breakfast
Tony does everything half an hour after Tim.
Ex 2 2 Tony listens to music at four forty-five. 3 Tony calls his friends at six thirty. 4 Tony goes to bed at eleven twenty.

7A What can you do?

Aims: To practice verbs of ability, and use *can, can't,* and *(not) very well*

Instructions: Ex 1 • Point to the first clue (2 across) and the accompanying picture, and ask students, *What verb goes here?* (*play [basketball]*). • Students write the word in the crossword. • Students figure out the verbs that go with the other pictures and add them to the crossword.

Ex 2 • Read the example sentence to students. • Show students how to make sentences and give examples about yourself and people you know (*I can sing very well. My sister can play tennis, but not very well. My mother can't use a computer.*). • Students make sentences about themselves or people they know.

Answer key: Ex 1 Across: 2 play 3 run 5 take 6 use
Down: 1 paint 3 ride 4 sew
Ex 2 Ss' own answers

7B An accident in the kitchen

Aims: To practice food vocabulary, and count and noncount nouns

Instructions: • Point to the two pictures. Explain that students have to find ten differences between the pictures, using the words from the box. • Read the example sentences to students. • Say, *Make sentences about carrots.* (*Picture A: There aren't any carrots. Picture B: There is a carrot.*) • Students write the sentences on the answer lines. • Students find seven more differences.

Answer key [order will vary]: 1 A There are some bananas. B There aren't any bananas. 2 A There are two onions. B There are three onions. 3 A There aren't any carrots. B There is a carrot. 4 A There isn't any cheese. B There is some cheese. 5 A There is an egg. B There are two eggs. 6 A There isn't any butter. B There is some butter. 7 A There is some milk. B There isn't any milk. 8 A There is some pasta. B There isn't any pasta. 9 A There isn't any bread. B There is some bread. 10 A There is some meat. B There isn't any meat.

7C Where am I?

Aims: To practice vocabulary for places in town, and use prepositions of location

Instructions: • Make a photocopy of the worksheet for each pair of students. • Cut the worksheets in half along the dotted line. • Arrange students in pairs. One student in each pair is Student A, the other is Student B. Give each student a Student A section or a Student B section.

Ex 1 • Show students that they both have pictures which represent places on a map of a town. • Explain that they have different places on the map in Ex 2. • Students match the places with the pictures.

Ex 2 • Explain that students are going to find out about the missing places on their maps. • Ask a Student A to read the places on his or her map (*bookstore, post office,* etc.) • Ask a Student B to read the places on his or her map (*train station, drugstore,* etc.) • Read the example question for Student A (*Excuse me, is there a bookstore near here?*) and ask a Student B to answer it. Show students how to find where the bookstore is on the map and label it. • Read the example question for Student B (*Excuse me, is there a train station near here?*) and ask a Student A to answer it. Show students how to find the train station on the map and label it. • Students take turns asking and answering the questions in pairs. They find the missing places on the map and write the labels.

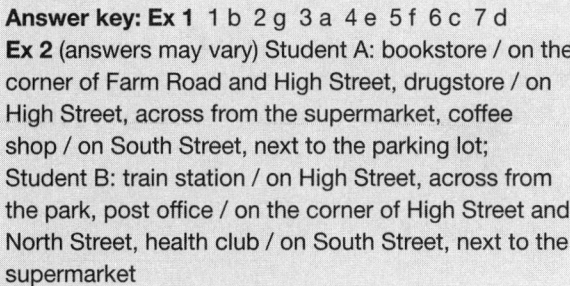

7D Consolidation 1 Motivator quiz: food

Aims: To review the language of the unit

Instructions: • Explain that this quiz is about food. Ask students to say, in their own words, the type of questions you find in a food quiz (*What dish with yellow rice is Spain famous for?*, etc.). • Read the first question to students and ask them to suggest the answer. • Students answer the rest of the questions individually. • Go through the correct answers with students (see Answer key). • Students figure out their score. • Congratulate students with a score of 7–8.

Answer key: 1 b) 2 c) 3 c) 4 c) 5 b) 6 c) 7 a) 8 a)

7D Consolidation 2 Categories

Aims: To review the vocabulary of the unit

Instructions: • Point to the first picture. Ask *What is it?* (*juggle*). • Show students the letters for *juggle* crossed out in the first set of scrambled letters. • Point to the letters that are not crossed out and ask students what word the extra letters make (*dance*). • Show students the example answers in the Abilities category in the table: *juggle* in the Picture word column, and *dance* in the Extra word column. • Students cross out the letters for the rest of the picture words, and write the words in the correct category. • They make extra words in the same category with the letters that are not crossed out. They add these words to the Extra word column.

Answer key: Abilities: juggle, dance / paint, sing / sew, cook / type, swim Food: grapes, orange / chicken, meat / carrot, rice

8A What's the weather like?

Aims: To practice weather vocabulary and the present continuous

Instructions: • Make a photocopy of the worksheet for each pair of students. • Cut the worksheets in half along the dotted line. • Arrange students in pairs. One student in each pair is Student A, the other is Student B. • Give each student a Student A section or a Student B section. • Show students that there is information about the weather in different parts of the world on the maps. • Explain that Student A has some information, and Student B has other information. • Point to the symbols on the maps and ask *What's the weather like?* (*It's raining. It's windy.* etc.). • Say the temperatures (*45 degrees, 64 degrees,* etc.). • Read the example questions for Student A (*What's the weather like in Sydney? What's the temperature?*) and ask a Student B to answer them (*It's raining and it's warm. It's 68 degrees.*). Show students how to add the weather symbol and the temperature to the map. • Read the example questions for Student B (*What's the weather like in Ankara? What's the temperature?*) and ask a Student A to answer them (*It's raining and it's warm. It's 64 degrees.*). Show students how to add the weather symbol and the temperature to the map. • Students take turns to ask and answer the questions in pairs. They complete the information in their maps.

Answer key: 1 Sydney, raining, warm, 68°; 2 Ankara, raining, warm, 64°; 3 Buenos Aires, sunny, hot, 95°; 4 Rio de Janeiro, cloudy, hot, 99°; 5 Moscow, snowing, freezing, 23°; 6 Beijing, snowing, freezing, 28°; 7 Madrid, cloudy, cold, 54°; 8 Rome, foggy, cold 45°; 9 New York, snowing, cold, 37°; 10 Mumbai, sunny, hot, 102°

8B Mixed-up sports

Aims: To practice sports vocabulary

Instructions: Ex 1 • Point to number 1. Ask students what sports word is hidden in the scrambled letters (*football*). • Show students the completed example for *football* in number 1 in the grid in Ex 2. • Students unscramble the rest of the words and write them in the grid.

Ex 2 • Show students that some squares in the grid are gray. • Students unscramble the letters from those squares to make two sports. • They complete the two photo captions.

> **Answer key: Ex 1** 1 football 2 volleyball 3 basketball
> 4 snowboarding 5 swimming 6 cycling 7 skiing
> 8 skateboarding
> **EX 2** a soccer b baseball

8C Homebody or party animal?

Aims: To practice *like, love, hate, prefer + -ing* and vocabulary for free-time activities

Instructions: Ex 1 • Give students time to read the text. • Show students the quiz and explain what it's about. • Explain that **extroverts** are people who like talking to people and going to parties. **Introverts** are people who prefer staying at home and listening to music or reading a book. • Read the first section of the quiz (*On weeknights . . .*) and ask, *What does Jason prefer? a) going to parties, or b) watching TV? (b).* • Show students the completed first example in Jason's column. • Students complete the table with the rest of Jason's choices. • Students then count the number of *a)* and *b)* answers. • They read the key to find out if Jason is an introvert or an extrovert.

Ex 2 • Students complete the quiz with their own choices. • They read what the quiz says about them. • They tell the class about themselves and Jason.

> **Answer key: Ex 1** Jason b), a), a), b), b), a); Jason has equal numbers of a) and b), so he's a balance of extrovert and introvert.

8D Consolidation 1 Motivator quiz: Sports

Aims: To review the language of the unit

Instructions: • Ask students to say, in their own words, the type of questions you find in a sports quiz (*Who won the World Series in 2010? How many people are there on a football team?* etc.). • Read the first question to students and ask them

to suggest the answer. • Students answer the rest of the questions individually. • Go through the correct answers with students (see Answer key). • Students figure out their score. • Congratulate students with a score of 7–8.

> **Answer key:** 1 b) 2 a) 3 c) 4 b) 5 c) 6 c) 7 b) 8 b)

8D Consolidation 2 I 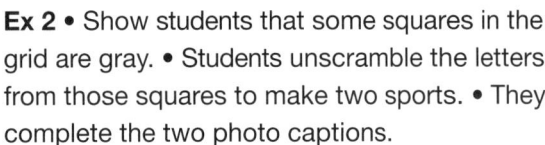 text messages

Aims: To review conversational phrases, and to role-play a conversation

Instructions: • Read the sentences in the box to students. • Show students the example answer in 1 (*Why don't we …*). • Ask students to find the correct phrase for 2, using the picture to help them. • Students complete the rest of the story. • Choose two students and assign a character (girl 1, girl 2) to each. • The two students read and role-play the conversation.

> **Answer key:** 1 f) Why don't we 2 g) not today
> 3 b) Let's go 4 d) How about 5 a) That's a good idea
> 6 c) You love 7 e) I have 462 text messages on my phone!

9A Who was the robber?

Aims: To practice using the simple past *be*

Instructions: Ex 1 • Read the extract from the newspaper article to students. • Explain that they are going to be detectives. They are going to figure out who took (robbed) the painting. • Ask individual students to read the speech bubbles for the different people at the house. • Make sure students understand when the picture was stolen: Alex Popov saw the picture in the dining room at 4:30, but when he went back to the room at 4:45, it wasn't there. So it was stolen between 4:30 and 4:45 in the afternoon. • Show students the plan of the house and the example answer for Alex Popov. • Students read the speech bubbles again. • They figure out where each person says he or she was between 4:30 and 4:45. • They draw a circle for each person on the map of the house and write the name in it. • Students figure out which person isn't telling the truth.

Ex 2 • Help students to answer the questions.
• Students say who they think took the painting and give reasons.

> **Answer key: Ex 1** Alex Popov – living room; Ian Grubber – swimming pool; James Cole – garage; Ana Popov – living room; Janice Cole – kitchen; Natasha Popov – kitchen; Lenny Rock – in front of the house; Jimmy Cole – garage
> **Ex 2** 1 Lenny Rock 2 Because nobody saw him between 4:30 and 4:45.

9B Where did they meet?

Aims: To practice prepositions of motion

Instructions: • Make a photocopy of the worksheet for each pair of students. • Cut the worksheets in half along the dotted line. • Arrange students in pairs. One student in each pair is Student A, the other is Student B. • Give each student a Student A section or a Student B section.

Ex 1 • Show students that they each have a map of a town. There is one person's route on the map: Armando for Student A and Monica for Student B. • Students trace the route of their person, then complete the text with the prepositions from the box.

Ex 2 • Student A reads the completed text about Armando's route to Student B. • Student B draws the route on his or her map.

Ex 3 • Student B reads the completed text about Monica's route to Student A. • Student A draws the route on his or her map.

Ex 4 • Students figure out where Armando talked to Monica.

> **Answer key: Ex 1** Student A: 1 out of 2 into 3 across 4 into 5 out of 6 past 7 into 8 out of 9 across 10 into 11 out of 12 along
> Student B: 1 out of 2 into 3 across 4 into 5 out of 6 into 7 out of 8 along 9 into 10 out of 11 along 12 past
> **Ex 4** Armando and Monica talked in the park: It's the only place they were in at the same time.

9C How are you?

Aims: To practice the simple past of regular verbs and adjectives of feeling

Instructions: Ex 1 • Read the verbs in the box to students. • Read the first text message to students. Show them that the verb *watch* has been added to the text message in the past tense. • Students complete the other text messages with the past tense forms of the verbs in the box. • Point to the first text message and ask, *How does this person feel?* • Students read the adjective (*sad*). • Repeat with the other messages • Point to Picture A and ask, *How does he feel?* (*angry*). • Ask, *Which message matches this picture?* (*7*). • Students match the rest of the pictures with the text messages.

Ex 2 • Show students the example answer for the past tense of *watch* in the grid. • Students complete the grid with the past forms from Ex 1 and find the mystery adjective in the gray squares.

> **Answer key: Ex 1** 1 watched 2 shouted 3 practiced 4 remembered 5 finished 6 missed 7 called;
> A7 B6 C5 D4 E1 F2 G3
> **Ex 2** 1 watched 2 shouted 3 practiced 4 remembered 5 finished 6 missed 7 called; the mystery adjective is *worried*

9D Consolidation 1 I know the answer!

Aims: To review conversational phrases and to role-play a conversation

Instructions: • Read the sentences in the box to students. • Show students the example answer in 1 (*There was a geography test at school.*). • Ask students to find the correct sentence for 2. • Students complete the rest of the conversation. • Choose two students and assign a character (mother, boy) to each. • The two students read and role-play the conversation.

> **Answer key:** 1 d) There was a geography test at school. 2 b) I only answered one question. 3 f) What was the question? 4 a) What did you say? 5 c) New York, of course. 6 e) The capital of the U.S. is Washington, D.C.

9D Consolidation 2 Construct a story!

Aims: To construct a story

Instructions: Ex 1 • Point to the pictures and ask questions such as, *Where is he?* and *What is he doing?* • Explain that students are going to construct the story of what happened last night. • Point to number 1 and ask, *How does the story start?* (*Last night my brother*). • Point to number 2 and ask, *How does it continue?* (*was asleep in his bed*). • Show students the line which links 1 and 2 (*Last night my brother* to *was asleep in his bed.*) • Students continue the story, drawing lines from one box to the next. • Choose students to read the story to the class.

Ex 2 • Read the three possible titles to students. • The Ss decide the best one.

Answer key: Ex 1 1 Last night my brother 2 was asleep in his bed. 3 At twelve o'clock 4 he walked 5 downstairs 6 and into the garden. 7 He climbed 8 the wall 9 and he started 10 to sing. 11 Then he stopped 12 and walked back to bed. 13 In the morning 14 he didn't remember 15 his concert!
Ex 2 The best title is *A musical adventure*

10A Get moving!

Aims: To practice vocabulary for means of transportation

Instructions: Ex 1 • Show students the picture for clue 1 down and ask, *What is it?* (*a plane*). • Students write *plane* in number 1 down in the crossword. • Students complete the rest of the crossword.

Ex 2 • Show students the six pictures (A to F). Explain that they are Ana's tickets and receipts. • Point to each one in turn and ask questions such as, *What means of transportation is it?* and *When did she travel?* • Ask, *Which is the first ticket?* (*D, City Bus*) • Show students the example answer 1 in the box. • Students number the rest of the tickets in date/time order.

Ex 3 • Students write about Ana's journey. They describe each part of the trip in the correct order.

Answer key: Ex 1 DOWN: 1 plane 2 boat 3 truck
ACROSS: 2 bike 3 train 4 bus
Ex 2 D 1 F 2 A 3 E 4 B 5 C 6
Ex 3 1 First, she went by bus to Heathrow Airport. 2 Then she went by plane to New York. 3 Then she went by taxi to the Madison Hotel. 4 The next day she went by boat around Manhattan Island. 5 On April 16 she went by train to Washington D.C. 6 The next day she went by plane to London.

10B A crazy vacation!

Aims: To practice general vocabulary

Instructions: Ex 1 • Make a photocopy of the worksheet for each student and cut it in half. • Give Part 1 to students. • Show the picture of the person to students. • Ask, *What is this person doing?* (*Going on a vacation*) • Explain that they are going to write a story about a vacation. • Point to number 1 and say, *Write a month. Any month.* • Students write a month on the line. • Continue with the other descriptions.

Ex 2 • Give each student a copy of Part 2. • Students copy their words from Part 1 into the text. • In pairs, students read the text about their crazy vacation to each other. • Choose a few students to read about their vacations to the class.

10C An active vacation!

Aims: To practice vocabulary for landforms, and to ask and answer questions about places, days, and activities

Instructions: • Make a photocopy of the worksheet for each pair of students. • Cut the worksheets in half along the dotted line. •Arrange students in pairs. One student in each pair is Student A, the other is Student B. • Give each student a Student A section or a Student B section.

Ex 1 • Show students that they both have a map. It shows what Jo did on his vacation. • Explain that Student A has details of some activities and some

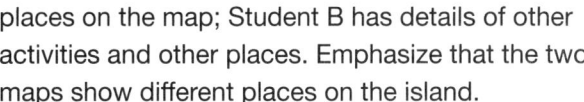

places on the map; Student B has details of other activities and other places. Emphasize that the two maps show different places on the island.
• Students complete the sentences in the diary, using the information on the map.

Ex 2 • Read the example questions for Student A (*What did Jo do on Friday?* and *Where did he go hiking?*) and ask a Student B to answer them. Show students how to complete the diary with the information. • Students ask and answer questions in pairs. The Student As complete the missing information in the diary.

Ex 3 • Read the example questions for Student B (*What did Jo do on Monday?* and *Where did he go biking?*) and ask a Student A to answer them. Show students how to complete the diary with the information. • Students ask and answer questions in pairs. The Student Bs complete the missing information in the diary.

> **Answer key: Ex 1–3** Monday: He went biking in the hills. Tuesday: He went sailing to the island. Wednesday: He played volleyball on the beach. Thursday: He went climbing in the mountains. Friday: He went hiking in the forest. Saturday: He went swimming in the river.

10D Consolidation 1 A bad vacation

Aims: To review conversational phrases and to role-play a conversation

Instructions: • Read the clues in the box to students. • Show students the example answer in 1 (*No, I didn't!*). • Show students that this is made from the words in clue *d)* in the box (*No / I / not*). • Ask students to find the correct set of words for 2 (*c*) *I / not / like / the food*). • Help students to make this into a sentence (*I didn't like the food.*). • Students complete the rest of the conversation. • Choose two students and assign a character (boy, his friend) to each. • The two students read and role-play the conversation.

> **Answer key:** 1 d) No, I didn't. 2 c) I didn't like the food. 3 f) I didn't swim in the ocean. 4 a) I didn't get to the top. 5 e) But I loved one thing. 6 b) I loved coming home!

10D Consolidation 2 A celebrity wedding

Aims: To review the simple past of regular and irregular verbs

Instructions: Ex 1 • Read the first paragraph from Part A, and point out the example answer for 1 (*met*). • Show students the past simple forms in the box. • Students complete Part A. • Repeat with Parts B and C.

Ex 2 • Point to number 1 and ask, *What is the simple past of "find"?* (*found*). • Students write *found* in the first row of squares. • Students complete the rows of squares with the past simple forms of the verbs. If they are not sure, they can find all the verbs in Ex 1. • Students read the mystery word and complete the sentence with it. • Students then circle every fourth word in the set of words below (*October, 10, is,* etc.). • Students read the mystery fact about Tom Cruise.

> **Answer key: Ex 1** 1 met 2 took 3 rode 4 gave 5 found 6 got 7 came 8 made 9 cut 10 sang 11 had 12 drove 13 left
> **Ex 2** 1 found 2 got 3 cut 4 rode 5 went 6 had
> The mystery word is fourth
> The mystery fact is: October 10 is Tom Cruise Day in Japan.

11A Which is the best laptop?

Aims: To practice understanding and working with technical information; to practice comparative and superlative adjectives

Instructions: Ex 1 • Point to the table and read the names of the computers to the students (*Orion 225, Star Mini,* etc.). • Ask questions about the computers, such as, *What is the screen size of the Alta 60N?* (*17 inches*) and *Is the QMT 894X expensive?* (*Yes, it is*). • Read the beginning of the text to students. Show them that *Star Mini* has been added in the first blank. • Students complete the rest of the text with the names of the computers.

Ex 2 • Ask a student to read the speech bubble for person number 1 to the class. • Students decide which is the best computer for this person.

• Students match the other people with the best computers for them.

11B What's the best sport for you?

Aims: To practice adjectives of quality, and comparative and superlative adjectives

Instructions: • Make a photocopy of the worksheet for each pair of students. • Cut the worksheets in half along the dotted line. • Arrange students in pairs. One student in each pair is Student A, the other is Student B. • Give each student a Student A section or a Student B section. • Show students that they both have a table comparing three exciting sports. • Explain that Student A has some information on their chart, and Student B has other information. • Read the example questions for Student A (*Is skateboarding more difficult than windsurfing?* and *Is skiing the most difficult sport?*) and ask a Student B to answer them. • Read the example questions for Student B (*Is skateboarding more dangerous than skiing?* and *Is skiing the most dangerous sport?*) and ask a Student A to answer them. • Show students the example answers in the first or second row in their respective charts. • Students take turns asking and answering the questions in pairs. They add the information to their worksheets.

Answer key:

	Skateboarding	Windsurfing	Skiing
Difficult	★	★ ★	★ ★ ★
Dangerous	★ ★	★	★ ★ ★
Exciting	★	★ ★	★ ★ ★
Expensive	★	★ ★	★ ★ ★
Fast	★	★ ★	★ ★ ★
Popular	★ ★ ★	★	★ ★

11C Clothesline

Aims: To practice vocabulary for clothes

Instructions: Ex 1 • Have students name different clothing items. • Point to the first word in the first chain. Show students that *dress* has been written in the boxes. • Point to the next box and ask, *What word goes here?* (*shirt*) • Students complete the rest of the chain.

Ex 2 • Show students the letters in the first circle. • Show that the letters can be made into two words, *boots* and *belt*. • Show students that the first letter of all the words is on the line. • Students make two clothes words from the other sets of letters.

11D Consolidation 1 Shopping for shoes

Aims: To review shopping for clothes and to role-play a conversation

Instructions: • Read the sentences in the box to students. • Show students the example answer in 1 (*The blue ones are the best.*). • Ask students to find the correct sentence for 2. • Students complete the rest of the conversation. • Choose three students and assign a character (the twins, salesclerk) to each. • The three students read and role–play the conversation.

11D Consolidation 2 The short adjective crossword

Aims: To review short adjectives, opposites, and comparative and superlative forms

Instructions: • Point to the first row in the table under the crossword and ask, *What is the opposite of* hard? (*easy*) • Show students the first column in the table, *Adjective*, and read the entry (*14 across*). • Show students the example answer in 14 across. • Repeat this process with the next two columns, *Comparative (easier, 9 down)* and *Superlative (easiest, 6 across)*. • Students complete the crossword.

> **Answer key:** ACROSS: 3 hotter 6 easiest 7 hot 8 biggest 10 better 11 big 12 good 13 dirty 14 easy DOWN: 1 hottest 2 dirtiest 4 best 5 dirtier 9 easier 10 bigger

12A Who's going to play?

Aims: To practice music vocabulary, and *going to* for future events

Instructions: • Make a photocopy of the worksheet for each pair of students. • Cut the worksheets in half along the dotted line. • Arrange students in pairs. One student in each pair is Student A, the other is Student B. • Give each student a Student A section or a Student B section. • Show students that they both have a poster about future music events at the Nitrogen Center. • Explain that Student A has some information and Student B has other information about the events. • Read the example questions for Student A (*What kind of music does Kimeva sing? How much are the tickets? When are The Slide going to be at the Nitrogen Center?*) and ask a Student B to answer them. Show students how to add the information to their worksheets. • Read the example questions for Student B (*When is Kimeva going to be at the Nitrogen Center? What type of music do The Slide play? How much are tickets for The Slide?*) and ask a Student A to answer them. Show students how to add the information to their worksheets. • Students take turns to asking and answering the questions in pairs. They add the information to their worksheets. (Note: Remind students that we write *April 12*, but we say *April twelfth*.)

> **Answer key:** Kimeva, R&B, June 12, Tickets $25; The Slide, heavy metal, April 30, Tickets $35; Chit Chat, pop, January 2, Tickets $45; San Diego Sound, Salsa, November 19, Ticket $55

12B The story machine

Aims: To practice adverbs and to construct a story

Instructions: • Point to the pictures on the page and ask questions such as, *Where is he?* and *What is he doing?* • Explain that students are going to construct the story of what happened at the ski jump. • Point to number 1 and ask, *How does the story start?* (*The skier started*). • Point to number 2, and ask, *How does it continue?* (*slowly*). • Show students the line which links 1 and 2 (*The skier started* to *slowly.*). • Students continue the story, drawing lines from one box to the next. • Choose students to read the story to the class. • Students write the story in the box.

> **Answer key:** 1 The skier started 2 slowly. 3 Then he went 4 very fast 5 and he jumped 6 very well. 7 He landed 8 well 9 The crowd shouted 10 loudly. 11 His 12 jump 13 was 14 a new 15 world record!

12C The talent show!

Aims: To practice *want* and *going to* + infinitive, and to role-play a conversation

Instructions: • Read the word clues in the box to students. • Show students the example answer in 1 (*I want to win this competition!*). • Show students that this is made from the words in clue *b*) in the box (*I / want / win / this competition*). • Ask students to find the correct set of words for 2 (a) *What / you / going / sing*). • Help students to make this into a sentence (*What are you going to sing?*). • Students complete the rest of the conversation. • Choose three students and assign a character (Luke, interviewer, + one student for the audience) to each. • The three students role-play the conversation.

> **Answer key:** 1 b) I want to win this competition! 2 a) What are you going to sing (, Luke?)? 3 d) I'm going to sing "Love hurts a lot." 4 c) You're going to hit the wasp! 5 e) I want to cry.

12D Consolidation 1 Motivator quiz: Music

Aims: To review the language of the unit

Instructions: • Explain that this quiz is about music. • Ask students to say, in their own words, the type of questions you find in a music quiz (*Where does reggae music come from?* etc.).

• Read the first question to students and ask them to suggest the answer. • Students answer the rest of the questions individually. • Go through the correct answers with students (see Answer key). • Students figure out their score. • Congratulate students with a score of 7–8.

Answer key: 1 b) 2 c) 3 a) 4 c) 5 c) 6 c) 7 a) 8 c)

12D Consolidation 2 Famous people . . . who aren't famous!

Aims: To practice understanding a text

Instructions: • Read the words in the first box to students. • Read the first part of the text.

Show students the example answer. • Students complete the rest of the text with the words from the box. • Show students the puzzle box. • Ask, *What is word 3?* (*games*). • Ask, *What is letter 1 of this word?* (*g*). • Students figure out the rest of the letters and read the word (*guitar*). • Students add the word to the final sentence and read the unusual fact about Shigeru Miyamoto. • Repeat with the second text.

Answer key: A Shigeru Miyamoto: 1 father 2 started 3 games 4 success 5 were 6 working
The missing word is *guitar*.
B Matt Groening: 1 in 2 draw 3 was 4 people 5 television 6 first 7 more
The missing word is *parents*.